ENGLISH THATCHED CHURCHES

By the same author

Thatching and Thatched Buildings
Thatched Buildings of Dorset
A History of English Country Sports
The Complete Guide to Living with Thatch

ENGLISH THATCHED CHURCHES

MICHAEL BILLETT

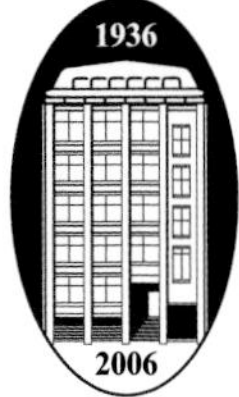

Robert Hale · London

First published in Great Britain 2006

ISBN-10: 0-7090-7985-0
ISBN-13: 978-0-7090-7985-9

Robert Hale Limited
Clerkenwell House
Clerkenwell Green
London EC1R 0HT

A catalogue record for this book is available from the British Library

2 4 6 8 10 9 7 5 3 1

Printed in China by New Era Printing Co. Ltd

To Helen

CONTENTS

Illustrations

PICTURE CREDITS

All photographs: H. Billett

LINE DRAWINGS

ACKNOWLEDGEMENTS

Many sources of information were used in compiling this book. In particular, I would like to thank the many writers of various church leaflets and guides which relate the history of some of the individual thatched churches. Also, I am grateful for the co-operation and help of the many churchwardens and clergy who kindly provided information.

INTRODUCTION

This book was written to enhance the pleasure of the many tourists and others who visit English country churches, particularly those with attractive thatched roofs. There are 100 of them and most are situated in remote villages, surrounded by beautiful countryside. Although many books have been written on parish churches and cathedrals, none has been solely devoted to those topped with picturesque thatch. This book therefore gives the general reader an insight into all the lovely thatched churches that still remain in England.

The thatchers who create their roofs deserve a special tribute because much of their skill depends purely on the judgement of their eyes and hands. No exact lines are predetermined and few technical measurements are taken, yet they stamp their own individual styles on the thatch with distinctive flourishes. This complements the work of the craftsmen and masons who built the churches. In their time, no architects as we know them today were available to calculate such things as loads and stresses.

The interiors of the churches also hold many treasures and offer a tour of discovery of early art and craftsmanship, such as fourteenth-century wall paintings, the skill of the Norman masons, the intricate work of the ancient carvers and the artistry of the stained-glass window designers. All churches are a mixture of various centuries and so give an insight into English as well as local history. Many were used for the social life of the village as well as for worship.

1

THATCH AND THE CHURCH

The widespread use of thatch dominated early church building and some of England's major churches, such as abbeys and cathedrals, were once thatched. For example, Sherborne Abbey in Dorset possessed a thatched roof in the fifteenth century and a thatched roof also once topped Gloucester Cathedral, until a fire in 1122 caused the burning roof to collapse into the nave, where the intense heat from the fire damaged the surfaces of some of the eleventh-century limestone piers. Discoloration marks caused by the fire still remain visible on the bases of some of the Norman piers.

Before the Norman Conquest, the early Saxons in the seventh century built their churches with timber and thatch, owing to the readily available supply of these materials from the heavily forested English landscape and marshland. The thatch material came from the water reeds that grew in the marshes; brushwood and turf were also used. Later, the Saxons introduced rye into England, so thatching straw also became available. The naves of early Saxon churches were always very narrow, no more than 20 feet wide. Thatched roofs require steep pitches to discharge rainwater quickly, and a narrow nave made it easier to construct this type of roof, with a pitch angle of around 50 degrees (see fig. 1). No Saxon churches survive in their entirety but many features, such as deeply splayed windows, sundials and stone crosses, still exist at many places across the country. However, few fonts survive. Most of our present dioceses date from the Saxon period, around AD 750. The local lord appointed the parish priest and this continued through the Middle Ages.

A church that retains a large proportion of Saxon work is St Andrew's at Greensted in Essex. It was originally thought to date to around AD 840 and therefore to be the only surviving example of a Saxon timbered church in England. The original massive vertical oak logs that form the walls of the nave still survive and they are tongued and grooved, with wooden pins securing them together. However, more recent tests suggest some of the

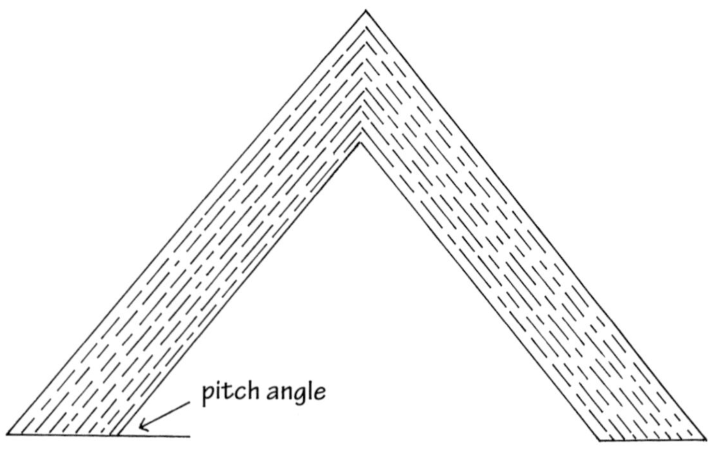

Fig. 1 Thatch pitch angle

work may be as late as 1063–1100 and the church has undergone many additions since. A thatched roof covered the church until the Tudors replaced it with tiles and also rebuilt the chancel in the early sixteenth century. The Victorians also carried out a restoration.

Stone obviously endures longer than timber and a Saxon church built with stone at an even earlier date, around AD 670, still stands at Escombe, near Bishop Auckland in County Durham; it has undergone only a few alterations, such as the insertion of windows. A thatched roof would once also have sheltered it, and an exhibition in the church has an illustration, designed by Christina Unwin, showing how the original thatched roof might have looked.

In East Anglia, there was a shortage of building stone but flints in all shapes and sizes were widely available and could be gathered from the fields. This led the later Saxons to build round towers with them in this region of England, possibly for defence against the marauding Danes. They were generally attached to their thatched churches, but a few were built separate from them; sometimes the only access to the tower was up to 10 feet above the ground. The absence of stone presented difficulties in the making of quoins for corners – with flints a near impossible task. The thick-walled round towers, bound together with lime and mortar, were the answer to this problem. Apsidal chancels were also often built.

In areas where stone was available, long-and-short work was used to make corner angles by laying quoins, with flat horizontal slabs alternating with tall vertical ones (see fig. 2). This allowed the late Saxons to construct

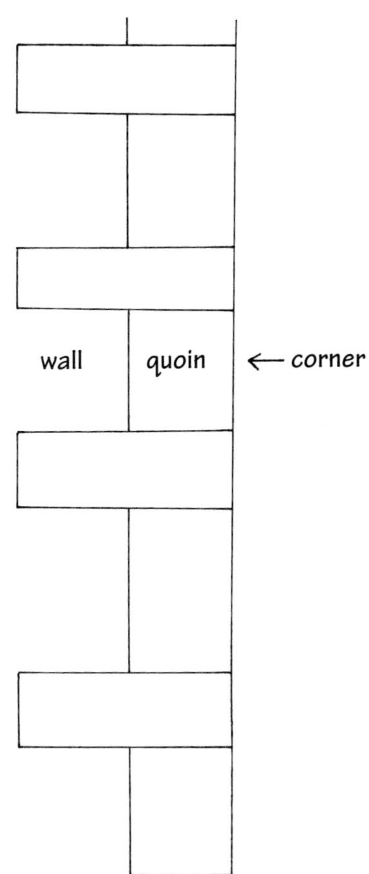

Fig. 2 Long-and-short work

square towers. The method was also used to make corners of windows and doors. Examples may be seen in various parts of the country. Saxon church walls were never buttressed. Interestingly, most displayed sundials on their south walls and stonemasons carefully carved them to make them decorative as well as functional. They divided the day into eight 'tides', often subdivided into 'half-tides' of a nominal one-and-a-half-hour duration.

After the Normans arrived in AD 1066 they often built on top of the Saxon round towers to increase their height. They also began to import limestone from Caen, in Normandy, and their masons started to build the corners of their churches, doorways and windows with it. It was often easier to do this than transport suitable workable stone from distant quarries in England. Oolitic limestone was also later widely used for building church walls, including buttresses. However, thatch was still retained on many churches. This may have been partly due to the fact that to support a heavy stone tiled roof, more substantial roof timbers would have been required. Thatch is very light and only needs relatively slim support.

In contrast to the Saxons, the Normans introduced primitive scratch dials that were based on 'seasonal hours', which varied in length depending upon the time of year. They measured the period from sunrise to sunset and were divided into twelve seasonal hours. They were often roughly scratched into stonework, with lines radiating out from a central hole in which a gnomon was placed. They were used on churches to inform the people, who were mainly illiterate, of the time of the next mass. The use of seasonal hours continued until about 1550 and parish mass was usually held at the end of the third hour. England, of course, was Catholic until Henry VIII broke from Rome in the sixteenth century.

Towards the end of the Norman period, between 1175 and 1200, church architecture underwent a transition from Norman or Romanesque, with rounded arches, to Early English, with pointed arches. This period lasted until around 1280. The Decorated Period that followed, using a new form of window tracery, lasted until about 1370 and was replaced by the Perpendicular Period, which had an upright form and dominated until around 1540. During the Middle Ages, the cruciform plan for churches became very popular, in contrast to the single- and two-cell types (see fig. 3).

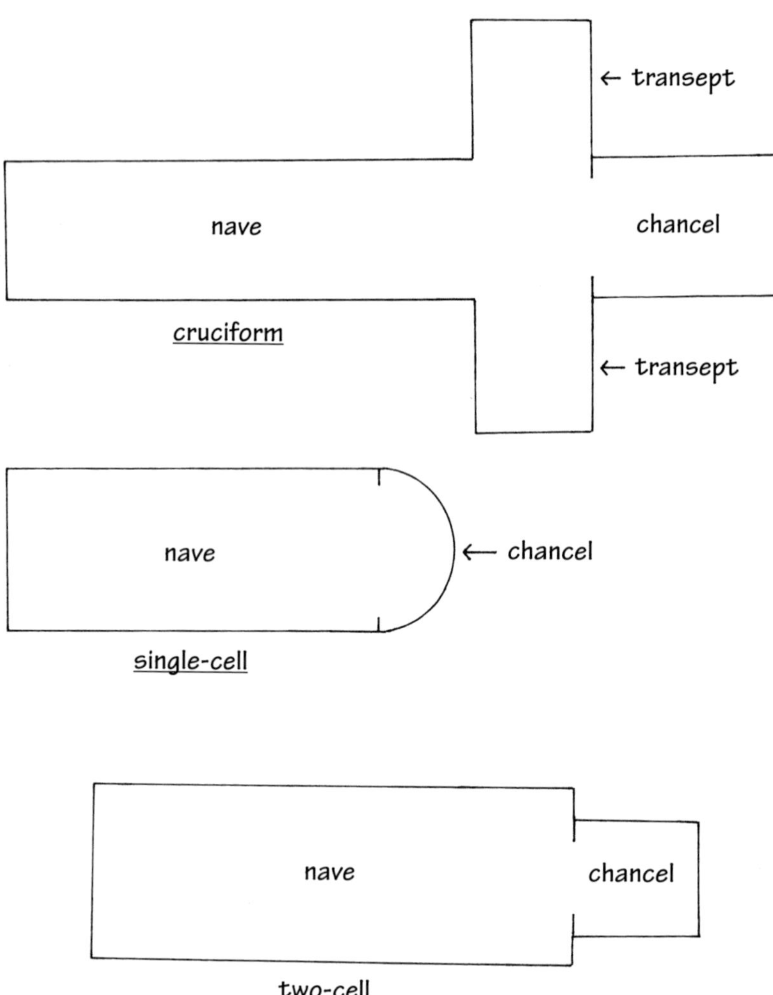

Fig. 3 Church layouts

The medieval Gothic period saw a frenzy of church building, particularly in the fifteenth century. On several churches, roofs were thatched as a temporary measure, and were coated with whitewash to increase their fire resistance. However, many were permanently thatched and some still remain today. In areas where flints were locally available, they continued to be used for wall building; after the fifteenth century, they were often knapped and squared for decorative purposes, rather than used in random form. Several churches also had thatched pyramid-shaped steeples. Wood continued to be used for bell-cotes, which were often complex in design to support the heavy weight of the bells. Wood gave versatility.

Little church building took place between the Reformation and the Restoration in 1660. But there was a growth of Nonconformist chapels and Quaker meeting houses, triggered by the widespread persecution these groups suffered for failing to accept the conditions laid down by the Act of Uniformity of 1662. They were anxious not to imitate established church architecture and built simple buildings, which were often thatched, or converted barns and cottages into places of worship. These types of buildings therefore served as a type of architectural camouflage, especially if they had a thatched roof that helped them to blend into the countryside. After the Toleration Act of 1689, chapel building could commence lawfully but in country areas the practice of converting thatched barns or cottages into chapels continued.

The building of churches resumed during the Georgian period, especially in towns and cities, and this spread in the Victorian era to country churches as well. Historians often accuse the Victorians of over-restoring a host of churches but it should be borne in mind that without their efforts, many would have passed into dilapidation and eventual destruction. This particularly applies to thatched churches, whose roofs only had limited life spans. Often churches were only partly thatched – either the nave or chancel. In some cases, too, the front elevation facing the road, was tiled, whilst the rear was thatched. The Victorians also continued the practice of adding thatched lychgates to churchyard entrances, as well as tiled ones. During funerals, they provided some measure of protection from the elements for the pallbearers, while they waited with the bier for the cleric to arrive for the burial service to lead the funeral procession. They marked the boundary between consecrated and non-consecrated ground.

The geographical distribution of the English thatched churches that survive in the twenty-first century varies enormously. There are many in Norfolk and Suffolk, owing to the abundance of water reeds from the fens and the lack of locally available stone. Hardly any survive in Hampshire and Berkshire, where once they were fairly abundant. Devon and Dorset, counties renowned for their thatched cottages and other buildings, can also claim very few thatched churches.

The number of thatched churches has steadily declined during the last two centuries; in 1840 there were approximately 270 in England but in the twenty-first century only about 100 survive. These consist of a mixture of Church of England, Roman Catholic, Congregational, Quaker, Baptist and British Orthodox. The main cause of the decline is neglect in the past and the high cost of thatch material today, together with the large area of a church roof to be covered. Depending upon the size, it costs between £50,000 and £100,000 to rethatch a church. Grants are sometimes available, but members of the parish also have to provide considerable sums. They often raise funds by encouraging donors to buy a bundle of reed for say £5, but many thousands of bundles are required to carry out a rethatch. Once thatch was a cheap roofing material but it is now almost a luxury product in comparison to more durable slates or tiles.

The three main types of thatch traditionally used on buildings, including churches, are water reed, combed wheat reed and long straw. Water reed, especially Norfolk reed, predominates in East Anglia. In the West Country, combed wheat reed is the most common. As suggested by its name, it is formed by passing wheat straw through a special comb to make the stalks parallel when bundled. Long straw is the same material but has been left in a more random loose array by not passing it through a comber. It is mainly found in the south of England and the Midlands. Unlike water and combed wheat reed, it is necessary to have extra fixing devices around the gable verges and eaves because of its looser nature (see fig. 4). The wheat used for thatching cannot be harvested with a combine harvester because it breaks up the straw into small pieces. A reaper and binder has to be used and this laborious method makes the product expensive. Owing to shortages and high prices, many reeds, including water and wheat reeds, are now imported from various parts of Europe and South Africa.

Thatch is fixed to the roof surfaces by various devices, including liggers, long lengths of split hazel that are pegged down over the thatch with spars, also usually made of hazel. Alternatively, especially with water reed, iron hooks are used to secure long rods of hazel or steel over the thatch layers. The ridges that cap thatched roofs are made of straw or sedge; water reed is not flexible enough to be bent over the apex. In the past, ridges were normally constructed flush to the roof surface and left

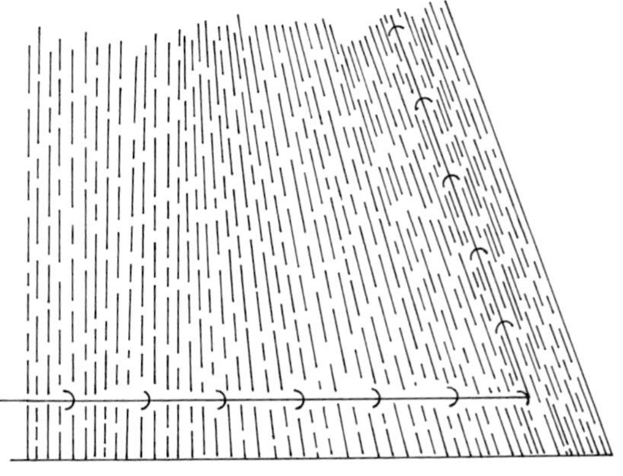

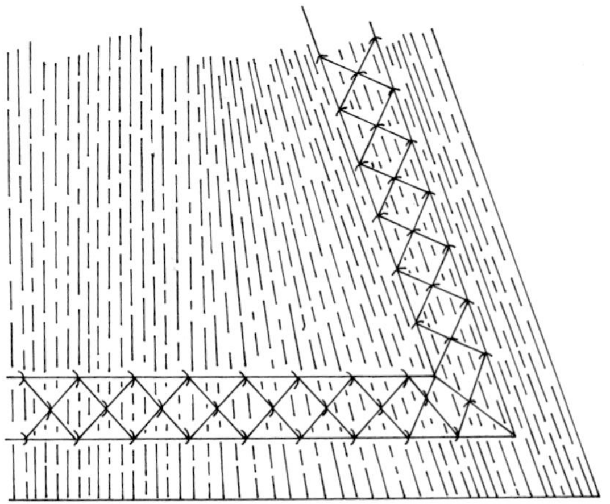

Fig. 4 Long straw finishes

plain, without ornamentation. Later, decorative block ridges came into vogue, especially in water reed areas. These were constructed by building up the ridge level about 3–4 inches above the roof surface, with the bottom edge cut into scallop and point shapes (see fig. 5).

Neglect, particularly of the ridge, often leads to the urgent necessity of a rethatch. Although a good quality reed thatch will last for up to seventy years, the ridge has to be replaced three or four times during this time. In addition, ridges are usually wire-netted because the fixings, such as spars and liggers are left exposed and subject to wind damage. Only good maintenance ensures longevity and prevents eventual leakage.

Fig. 5 Thatched ridge ornamentation

A major reason for roof failure is loss of thatch material brought about by the ravages of time, resulting in a reduced depth of thatch. This erosion may result from decay and woodworm in the hazel fixing rods, which loosens their tension below the thatch surface, or corrosion of the iron hooks that keep the thatch tightly packed to avoid roof slippage. Wind damage to the eaves and birds pulling out thatch for nesting, or searching for insects and grain aggravate the problem. Many of the thatched churches that survive today do so as the result of the efforts of such bodies as the Churches Conservation Trust, the Historic Churches Preservation Trust, the National Trust, English Heritage and the Historic Chapels

Bird damage to thatch, Loughwood Meeting House, Dalwood, Devon

Trust. The latter was founded in 1993 to cover Roman Catholic, Protestant and Nonconformist buildings.

However, many thatched churches have proved uneconomic to repair and alternative roofing materials have been substituted. There is a host of examples; the following is just a small selection covering a range of religious denominations. In 1701, at Brant Broughton in Lincolnshire, Thomas and Sarah Robinson donated a small thatched barn for use as a Quaker meeting house. It still stands today but pantiles now replace the thatch on the roof. Also in Lincolnshire, St Mary's church at Cowbit has endured an interesting history of roof changes. The church dates from the fourteenth century and the nave was originally thatched. Later, slates were substituted and now lead covers the roof; once the tower also had a conical thatched roof. At Soham, in Cambridgeshire, a rented thatched wooden barn, with an earthen floor, hosted the first Baptist meetings held there in about 1770. In 1783, a more permanent church was constructed using a mixture of steel, clay, brick and thatch. It has since been demolished and the new Baptist church built on its site is not thatched.

In Norfolk, a thatched roof sheltered the nave of St Helen's church at Ranworth, until a fire broke out in 1963. At nearby Belaugh, St Peter's church had thatch until the nineteenth century, when tiles replaced it.

Also in Norfolk, at Great Melton there were once two medieval churches unusually in a single churchyard. One of them was thatched but in 1873 it was demolished, leaving only its west tower. A slate roof covers the surviving church, All Saints. In Suffolk, St Thomas à Becket's church at Great Whelnetham remained thatched for eight centuries until the nineteenth century.

Finally, it is worth mentioning a former thatched chapel that unfortunately collapsed after a fire broke out during renovation in October 1976. It was known as Ebenezer Chapel and it formed a good example of a simple rural Methodist place of worship of the early nineteenth century. A large stone memorial marks the spot where it once stood. It is in the hamlet of Cripplestyle, about 1 mile south-west of Alderholt in Dorset, off the B3078. The memorial has inscribed on it the following history of the chapel:

> This was the site of Ebenezer Old Chapel built by the inhabitants of this hamlet with their own hands in 1807 of clay, heather, wood and thatch. It had to be extended twice to meet the needs of the families whose cottages were scattered over a wide area of the surrounding heathland. From 1888 having been replaced with a new brick built chapel it was only used annually for Divine worship but was revered and cherished not only for its

Ebenezer Chapel memorial, Cripplestyle, Dorset

simple beauty but as a memorial to the faith of those who conceived and built it. Despite efforts for its preservation it collapsed in October 1976. Praise to God the witness which began here still continues.

The new brick chapel referred to was built some 300 yards to the north but without a thatched roof, and is not in use as a chapel today.

2

THATCH AND THE CLERGY

In addition to churches, thatch may also be found on other ecclesiastical buildings, such as priests' houses, clergy houses and rectories. A good example of a medieval thatched priest's house stands at Muchelney, in Somerset, built in 1308. It is now cared for by the National Trust; it is opposite the parish church of St Peter and St Paul. The house is occupied and furnished by tenants and has restricted opening hours. Another fourteenth-century thatched clergy house stands at Alfriston, in East Sussex, also opposite the parish church. It was built by monks from the nearby abbey, in the form of a Wealden hall house. However, there is some doubt as to whether the parish priest ever lived there. The National Trust also now cares for it; it was the first building they purchased, for £10 in 1896.

Thatched priest's house, Muchelney, Somerset

As well as priests' houses, tithe barns were also frequently thatched, such as the magnificent huge one at Abbotsbury, in Dorset, and the impressive one at Paston, in Norfolk. They once stored the tithes (the one-tenth of the grain produce of a parish) that were levied to support the clergy and the Church. This form of taxation became compulsory in England during the tenth century and continued for many centuries before gradually dying out. Tithes in kind were abolished by law in 1836.

Thatched rectories were also much in vogue, and may still be found scattered around the country. Many have now been converted into private homes. A particularly beautiful one in a *cottage orneé* style, now privately owned, stands at Winterborne Came, in Dorset. It was formerly the home of William Barnes, the Dorset dialect poet who was rector for over twenty years during the second half of the nineteenth century at the nearby tiny Perpendicular church of St Peter. A few convents were also thatched and a former eighteenth-century one, now a private home, still survives in woodland on the Stourhead Estate, in Wiltshire. It once contained painted panels depicting nuns dressed in the clothes of the various orders.

The clergy were well aware of the risk of fire in thatched churches. During the seventeenth and eighteenth centuries they often displayed insurance plaques, called firemarks, on the exterior walls to inform the fire brigade they had paid the necessary premium. This reassured the fire offices, who employed and maintained the firemen and fire engines, that they would be paid if they attended a fire. The mark indicated the policy number and which particular fire brigade was responsible for it. The two main insurers were the Phoenix Fire Office, founded in 1682 and the Sun Fire Office, founded in 1710. The former's emblem was a phoenix rising from the flames and the latter's a sun with rays radiating around its face.

Many clergy also allowed fire hooks to be kept in their churches for their parishioners to use for quickly tearing away burning thatch from a roof. Even if the church itself was not thatched, fire hooks were still kept there so that villagers living in nearby thatched cottages could get them in the event of a cottage fire. The huge fire hooks were attached to wooden poles about 14 feet long, and they were heavy and cumbersome to handle. Oak was often selected for the poles because it did not ignite as easily as most other woods. It became the practice to fix iron rings to the eaves of churches and houses so that ropes could be inserted through them to assist in pulling up and supporting the weight of the fire hook. Examples of old fire hooks may still be seen in the church of St Mary the Virgin at Eaton Bray, Bedfordshire, St John the Baptist's church at Bere Regis, Dorset, and

Fire hooks at St John the Baptist, Bere Regis, Dorset

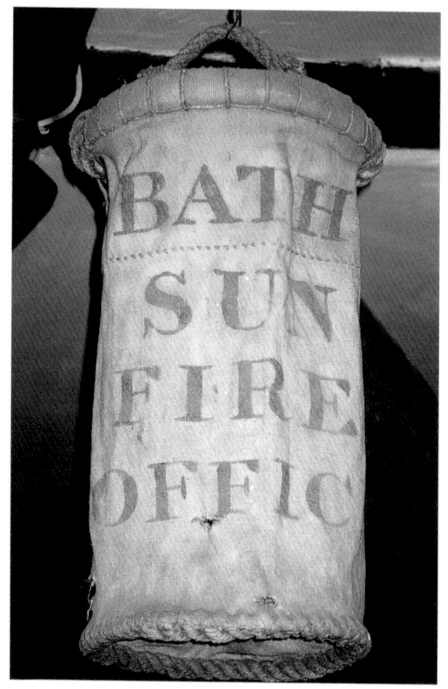

Canvas fire bucket at St Mary, Puddletown, Dorset

St Mary's church at Ivinghoe, Buckinghamshire, even though the churches themselves are not thatched. In addition, St Mary's church at Puddletown, in Dorset, still contains several old canvas fire buckets. They have been hanging there since 1805, when they were first issued by the Bath Sun Fire Office. This particular office was established in 1776 and its business transferred to the Sun Fire Office in London in 1839. The church lies close to thatched cottages in the village.

The clergy once allowed animals and even birds into churches; most churches were close to rural life. In the fourteenth century, perches were often provided inside some of them so that visiting clergy could chain up their falconry hawks during services; hawking was commonplace. Shepherds also brought their sheepdogs into the church and stray dogs also often crept in. The clergy provided iron dog tongs or churchwardens' staves to remove disruptive animals and stray ones. Some churches still have them, such as the thatched St Mary's church at Coney Weston, in Suffolk. Several Nonconformist churches, such as the Quaker meeting house at Come-to-Good, in Cornwall, provided thatched stabling for their members' horses. An example of a linhay stands at the Spiceland Quaker meeting house at Uffculme, in Devon. Later, the Victorian era produced a legion of 'sporting' parsons who indulged in fox hunting and other country sports.

Benches started to appear in a few churches at the beginning of the fourteenth century but they did not come into general use until much later. Until the early sixteenth century, the congregation nearly always stood or knelt before the priest; the nave was usually kept bare with no benches for them to sit on. One advantage of this with a thatched church was that if the roof caught fire and collapsed into the nave, there were no wooden benches to provide additional fuel for the blaze.

When Henry VIII became Supreme Head of the Church of England in 1534, Protestantism was established in England, and was carried on later in a moderated form by his daughter, Elizabeth I. In Henry's reign, rood lofts, galleries above the chancel screen, were pulled down, and the stone newel stairs which led to them so that candles could be lit on the rood beam were closed. The rood, above the screen, depicting the Crucifixion, flanked by the Virgin and St John the Evangelist, was also often taken down. Doom paintings commonly painted on the tympanum or on the wall above the chancel arch, were also removed. These showed the terrible prospect of the Judgement Day, when the graves would give up their dead for the souls to be weighed by the Archangel Michael. Angels received the good into bliss, whilst devils forced the bad into the fiery mouth of Hell. Instead of these Catholic images, Henry VIII substituted the royal coat of arms on or beneath the chancel arch to represent the connection between the monarch and the church and to indicate the divine right of kings. In some churches, the royal arms were placed elsewhere in the nave and during the Victorian restoration many more were resited.

The Reformation saw most wall paintings being covered with lime-wash to obliterate any images that related to 'Papist' idolatry. Cromwell's fanatical iconoclasts continued the task with zeal during the seventeenth century. Before the Reformation, church interiors were vividly coloured and painted with biblical scenes, to teach the scriptures to local folk who could not read and to warn them of their fate if they sinned against God. The English language was also substituted for Latin in church services, and sermons eventually became longer. The Book of Common Prayer was introduced in the reign of Edward VI, the son of Henry VIII. The liturgical change and the altered form of services, without the Catholic mass, led to the spread of benches for sitting. In the West Country, the bench ends were usually made square but in Norfolk and Suffolk they were given elaborately carved 'poppyhead' finials. A favourite motif for these was the fleur-de-lis and some also had carved images of saints, with their attributes or symbols. Others displayed carvings of animals and grotesques. In the seventeenth and eighteenth centuries, box pews were also introduced to reduce draughts and give more comfort. They were much favoured by richer members of the community, as they provided more privacy, which they paid for. In thatched churches, hassocks for kneeling were often made with the same reed that was used to thatch the roof.

Later, the solidity, strict moral code and sense of duty of the Victorians ensured regular church attendance. Regular prayer also became a feature of the workplace, as shown in a copy of a staff notice that came to light after an office building was demolished in 1852. Two of the relevant clauses state:

1. Godliness, Cleanliness and Punctuality are the necessities of good business.
2. Daily prayers will be held each morning in the main office. The clerical staff will be present.

The Victorian gentry continued the tradition of sending the eldest son into the army and the second into the Church. More livings became available as a result of the largest increase in church building since the Normans. The rector usually remained class conscious, continuing the practice of burying the more important near to the church on the south, sunny side of the churchyard, whilst the less important and the so-called 'shady' characters were buried away from the church on the north side. Throughout history, the very important and famous were usually entombed inside the church and the closer to the altar the more important they were.

In the Victorian period and early twentieth century, industrialists started to manufacture prefabricated church or chapel kits in corrugated iron. These were available in several different sizes, of varying price, and could be delivered and erected on the purchaser's pre-prepared foundations. For example, a kit 40 by 20 feet cost about £100 for delivery to the nearest rail or wharf of the buyer or about £137 for delivery and erection. The kits were supplied by various Manchester ironmongers and could also be ordered from Boulton and Paul of Norwich. There were several London manufacturers, including William Cooper Ltd in the Old Kent Road and J. E. Humphreys in Blackman Street and Borough Road Station. Several chapels and churches constructed from these kits are still used for regular worship.

The 'drumming' noise when it rained heavily on a corrugated iron roof often made it difficult for the congregation to hear the sermon. The problem was overcome in several churches by replacing the iron roof with a thick layer of thatch, which has excellent sound-deadening properties. All Saints at Little Stretton, in Shropshire, and St Felix chapel at Babingley, on the Royal Sandringham Estate, are two such churches.

Many clergy encourage a model of a thatched stable scene depicting the nativity at Christmas.

Thatch nativity stable scene

The importance of baptism in Christian life means that every church possesses a font, a large number dating from the twelfth and thirteenth centuries. Font derives from the Latin for fountain or spring and, in ecclesiastical terms, the water of baptism. Fonts are situated in the west end of the church as they denote a Christian's entry into the Church. Purbeck marble became a favourite material for their manufacture and was mined from two narrow seams on the Isle of Purbeck, in Dorset. It is not a true marble, although it could be highly polished, but a fossilized limestone derived from freshwater snails. In the thirteenth century, it was transported all over England and also into Normandy.

The octagonal shape of the font is significant. God created the earth in seven days and the eighth is the Day of Judgement or Second Coming, which signifies regeneration. The octagonal font symbolizes the place of regeneration or rebirth, as baptism gives entry into the Church. Fonts are frequently carved with scenes and symbols of Christian belief, although the iconoclasts damaged many after the Reformation, in their zeal to ban the use of images in religious worship. Fonts were frequently lined with lead to stop holy water seeping away into the stone or marble. This allowed the same water to be used over and over again. Incidentally in 1236, it was ordered that all fonts should be locked with a cover, to prevent sanctified water being stolen and used for occult or mystical purposes. Staples were commonly fitted to secure a metal bar across the top of the lid.

Finally, pulpits were installed much later than fonts, generally in the fifteenth or early sixteenth century. After the Reformation, when services took place in English, preaching assumed a new importance. In the seventeenth and eighteenth centuries, the 'three-decker' pulpit came into favour, raising the preacher well above the congregation, including even the tallest box pews, which he could then see into. A tester or sounding-board above resonated the preacher's voice around the nave. The parish clerk normally sat on the lower tier, prayers and lessons were issued from the second and the sermon from the top. Sermons often rambled on for long periods and to remind the preacher of the time, an iron stand with an hourglass was installed in a prominent position; one can be seen in the thatched church of All Saints at Edingthorpe, in Norfolk. Unfortunately, the Victorians seemed to dislike the 'three-deckers' and frequently cut them down in size. Lecterns were then favoured to read the lessons. Both old and new ones were commonly fashioned in the shape of an eagle, which symbolized St John the Evangelist and the possibility of renewal by soaring into the presence of Christ. The wings of the eagle were an appropriate support for the gospels.

3

GAZETTEER

BEDFORDSHIRE

Keysoe Row – Baptist Church

The delightful quaint church is situated in Keysoe Row East, about 8 miles north of Bedford on the B660. It was founded in 1808, after its conversion from a late eighteenth-century barn. The church is one of only two thatched churches in Bedfordshire.

A reed thatched roof shelters the small brick building. Wire netting protects the thatch, and cross-rods, between liggers, ornament the level ridge. The church lies sideways to the road and the thatch finishes with

Baptist Church, Keysoe Row, Bedfordshire

a half-hip over the solitary upper window facing the road. This window, and all the other plain-paned glass windows, are painted white. In contrast, the central entrance door is brown and a narrow garden borders both sides of it, with a well-kept lawn in front. The churchyard lies on the far side of the building and is sheltered by trees. A low brick wall runs parallel to the road and abuts the front corner of the church. A stone plaque set in the wall greets visitors with the following message:

A Friendly Word
A Kindly Smile
A Helpful Act
And Life's Worthwhile

The interior is a simple room with all its walls painted white. The pastor addresses his congregation from the pulpit in front of the row of plain, long pews that fill the church. Antique lamps suspended from the ceiling radiate a homely atmosphere for those attending the regular services. The thatched private residence that stands beside the church may have once been the home of the pastor.

Interior of Baptist Church, Keysoe Row, Bedfordshire

Roxton – Congregational Church

This rustic thatched church, with an unusually attractive design, may be found in the village of Roxton, about 8 miles north-east of Bedford. It lies off the A421, near where it links with the A1. The River Ouse flows to the south of the village.

The history of the church is interesting. It was built as a barn, converted at the beginning of the nineteenth century, officially becoming a place of worship in 1808. Until then, the only place of worship in the village was the Anglican church. Some villagers preferred to attend Nonconformist meetings, but the nearest church was situated at St Neots, about 5 miles away. This entailed a tedious journey by horse or horse and cart. So Charles J. Metcalf, a local landowner, who lived at nearby Roxton Park, decided to establish his own Congregational church in the village by converting his barn.

No permanent minister was at first appointed; services were held by visiting preachers and laymen, including Metcalf himself. However, in 1823 it was decided to appoint a full-time minister and later Metcalf added two wings to the church, one for use as a day school and the other as a Sunday school.

The wheat straw roof has a wire-netted ridge, decorated on its lower

Congregational Church, Roxton, Bedfordshire

edge with scallops. An eyebrow window in the thatch illuminates a gallery inside the church. Three little turrets emerge through the apex of the roof, with neat thatch aprons below. A rethatch took place in the 1990s, together with other substantial repairs. English Heritage contributed about a third of the total renovation cost of £93,000, the rest coming from local contributions and especially from fifteen regular members of the congregation, who worked incessantly to raise funds. Picturesque split tree trunks, purely ornamental, support the wide overhanging thatch eaves of the church. This gives the impression of a rustic verandah surrounding the perimeter of the church. Some of the trunks have rustic struts to emulate a form of wooden tracery.

The white walls are of roughcast set on brick foundations. The church is T-shaped; the front is the main meeting room, whilst two further rooms at the back form the top of the T. One of these is now used as a kitchen store. The ends of the T are rounded. There are a total of four porches around the church, one of which is exotic and grotto-like. It is lined with twigs, with conifer cones decorating its ceiling and the tops of its walls.

The doors of the church are of Gothic form, with some metal ornamentation. The windows are also of Gothic form and multi-paned; two are

Exotic porch of Congregational Church, Roxton, Bedfordshire

of stained glass and the others plain. One of the stained-glass windows shows St Francis feeding the birds; it is in memory of Philip Charles Bath, 1916–89.

Simple rustic benches stand inside the church, on the south side of which Metcalf had his pew. Stairs lead up to a gallery in the first bay. Outside there is a well-cared-for garden with trees, hedges and a rose garden. The south wing of the church offers good views over Roxton Park, where Metcalf lived. The building is in keeping with others in the village that are thatched, with one also having timber supports below the eaves.

CAMBRIDGESHIRE

Long Stanton – St Michael's Church

This small, thatched thirteenth-century church is situated about 7 miles north-west of Cambridge and is best accessed by taking the B1050 off the A14. If it is locked, the key can be borrowed from a key-holder next door. St Michael's has not been in regular use as a place of worship since 1954 and the Churches Conservation Trust has cared for it since 1975. It

St Michael, Long Stanton, Cambridgeshire

remains a consecrated building and weddings are still sometimes held there. The dedication to St Michael took place in 1217.

The porch, which has a niche added in the fifteenth century, and the nave were both rethatched in the summer of 2000. The previous roof had given seventy years of service. Messrs Dobson Brothers of Huntingdon carried out the rethatch, using 4,000 bundles of Norfolk reed and completing the work in four weeks. The main ridge and the porch were ornamented with scallops and points. The chancel too was once thatched, but it was tiled during Victorian restoration.

The walls are constructed of brown rubble stone and two buttresses support the west wall, positioned closely either side of the fourteenth-century west window. A double bell-cote with arches stands above the west window, but surprisingly contains no bells. Thieves stole them, including one from the fifteenth century, during a dark night in 1969. It remains a mystery how they were removed from their housing, lowered 70 feet to the ground and silently spirited away.

The interior of the church is plain, with limewashed walls, and the nave consists of four bay arches with two aisles. The abaci and bases of the piers alternate in shape from round to octagonal, and the arches are double-chamfered. In its long history, many generations have carved their initials and dates into the stonework. The dates range from the fifteenth to the eighteenth century. Another small carving depicts the old village windmill. The curved nineteenth-century ceiling is wooden boarded. Tiles cover the floor and there are plain open benches in the nave. Around the 1850s the rector, William Cecil, an enthusiastic amateur inventor, devised a small concealed stove to keep him warm on cold winter days. Prior to becoming rector, he designed the first gas engine.

A double-chamfered arch leads into the chancel, whose prime possession must be its superb thirteenth-century double piscina in the south wall. Its two round intersecting arches with tracery are similar to those in Jesus College Chapel in Cambridge. The east window contains Victorian glass with a date of 1883. A fifteenth-century brass inscription on the chancel step commemorates Thomas Burgoyne, a former patron of the church and lord of the manor. It offers the following philosophical message: 'As you are now so once was I; as I am, so will you be.'

Many Americans visit the church, as it became a model for at least two churches in the United States, one in Philadelphia, named St James the Less, which was built in 1846, and the other in South Dakota. The peaceful churchyard sits back a little from the road and just inside the entrance gate may be found St Michael's well. Steps lead down to it and it has a

St Michael's well, Long Stanton, Cambridgeshire

brick vault and iron railings. It dates from medieval times and the spring-fed well was used for baptisms until the 1880s.

Rampton – All Saints

The parish church lies about 2 miles north-east of Long Stanton and can be reached via the A14 and B1050 roads. On arrival at Rampton, the church proves a little difficult to find. It lies hidden off the main road but a church notice board by the roadside indicates the well-trodden path leading to it. The path rambles alongside a large house until it reaches a circle of yew trees that surround the church. The church is usually open, and there are an old and a new churchyard.

All Saints has a variety of roof types: reed thatch ornamented with a pointed ridge covers the nave, whilst tiles shelter the chancel and slates the porch. The square bell tower has gargoyles and narrow lancet windows below the louvred bell-opening, and dates from the thirteenth century. The tower is crenellated, with a weather-vane on top. The thatched roof abuts the bell tower and the thatch appears to be shallow.

The walls of the church consist mainly of stone rubble and parts date

All Saints, Rampton, Cambridgeshire

Interior of All Saints, Rampton, Cambridgeshire

from the thirteenth century. However, many additions and alterations have been made during the intervening centuries. Scratch dials are found on the south wall. The window spaces in the north wall of the chancel and nave were inserted in the early fourteenth century to increase the amount of light entering the interior. The east window was renewed in 1924 but the window in the Lady Chapel of the Virgin and Child dates from the fifteenth century. Most other windows are plain glass leaded lights but some have small quatrefoils with stained glass. The red brick porch, laid in English bond, dates from the late seventeenth or early eighteenth century.

Inside, a lovely dark moulded queen-post roof of the fifteenth century supports the thatched roof over the nave. The octagonal pillars, with moulded capitals in the south arcade, are of the thirteenth century. However, the one nearest the bell tower is fifteenth century, along with the bell tower arch. The tower contains six bells, two of which are medieval. The late rector, Revd Havers, donated the treble one in memory of his brother who died on HMS *Dasher* during the Second World War. The colourful bell ropes at the base of the tower are visible from the nave.

Plain benches several centuries old may be found in the church. Stone fragments from Saxon coffin lids are set in the north wall of the nave and others may be found set in the east wall, each side of the altar. The octagonal limestone font comes from the twelfth century, whilst the pulpit with its carved oak panels and sounding-board is from the seventeenth century. The north window recess beside the pulpit contains a niche. A wall painting of St Christopher, the patron saint of travellers, may be found on the north wall, directly opposite the porch entrance. Its faded appearance is due to its fifteenth-century origin. Traces of other ancient paintings are also visible along the same wall.

The chancel arch was enlarged in the fourteenth century but the Norman shafts still remain. Tiles cover the chancel floor and plain wooden planks form the chancel ceiling. The double piscina with fluted basins originated from the thirteenth century. Also in a chancel recess, beneath an ogee arch, lies the tomb of a member of the de Lisle family, who were once lords of the manor. The effigy, much worn by the ravages of time, shows the thirteenth-century crusader knight, dressed in full armour. It is thought that he once attempted to build a fortified stronghold on nearby Giant's Hill, an ancient earthwork, but he was defeated in battle before the castle could be constructed. However, there are a moat and mound there. The site lies to the east of the churchyard.

CORNWALL

Come-to-Good, near Feock – Quaker Meeting House

This picturesque Society of Friends meeting house is on an unnumbered road. It lies south of the A39; if one is travelling from nearby Truro, it is reached by turning off at Playing Place village, following the signpost to Feock and King Harry Ferry. About a mile down this road take a right turn at the crossroads, which leads to Come-to-Good. There is only limited parking at the meeting house, which is left open daily for visitors. Meetings for worship take place every Sunday morning at 10.30.

The name Feock derives from that of an obscure saint, who probably lived in the seventh or eighth century, whilst the enchanting name Come-to-Good possibly originates from the Cornish *cwm-ty-coit*, 'the coomb by the dwelling in the wood'. Alternatively, it may have come from a sarcastic reference to the place where the Quakers met. The meeting house, which is a Grade 1 listed building, rests in a hollow down a secluded lane, amidst a green and trees. Unfortunately, the proximity of the trees encourages the formation of moss on the thatched roof.

Quaker Meeting House, Come-to-Good, Cornwall

The building dates from 1710. It was built of cob and roofed with deep combed wheat reed thatch topped by a plain ridge, ornamented with liggers and cross-rods. The original cost was £68 18s 3d. The building was originally very small, 20 by 27 feet, but it has since been extended. A catslide thatched roof, supported by rustic timbers, was first added at the east end to shelter a linhay, with its roof sweeping effortlessly to join the main thatch. It served as a stable for the churchgoers' horses and was added in the early nineteenth century. In 1967 a thatched porch or lobby was added on to the west end; originally the entrance was in the centre of the south side. There is also a flat-roof extension to the rear used for a children's group. As is normal with cob, whitewash protects the thick outer walls; the sturdy buttresses were added later. Whitewash is used because it allows the cob to 'breathe' and dry. Shuttered casement windows on the south side, with leaded diamond panes, further enhance the rustic charm of the building. They were installed in 1710 and were obtained from another building at Penelewy Barton in Feock parish. There are no windows on the north side. The shutters are painted green, as is the porch door, which leads into an inner lobby, with a folding door opening into the meeting house.

The simple interior offers a west gallery that was constructed in 1717 for £15 10s 0d. A rear window admits light to it. The gallery is supported

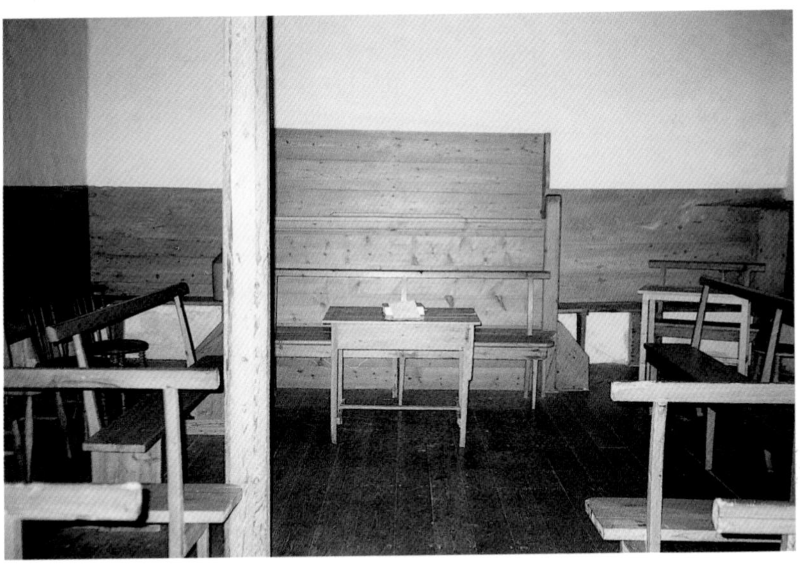

Interior of Quaker Meeting House, Come-to-Good, Cornwall

by timber posts that previously served as a ship's mast, and a narrow rear staircase leads up to it. The latter is newer than the gallery; the stairs were once positioned on the front side, but were changed in the nineteenth century. The front of the gallery displays a central wooden clock, to the far right of which is the blocked doorway of the former gallery entrance. The meeting house has no ceiling and the underside of the thatch may be seen towering above the plain pine benches below. The benches have open backs; some are arranged sideways and others face the front. There are also some individual chairs. All give a view to the raised pine stand at the east end where gifted members can be heard. The floor consists of exposed pine planks.

George Fox, founder of the Society of Friends, was imprisoned in Launceston Castle during his visit preaching throughout Cornwall in 1656. At that time, thatch was widespread throughout the county but like Come-to-Good, the surviving thatched buildings are now mainly found in the more sheltered southern spots of Cornwall.

DEVON

Dalwood – Loughwood Meeting House

This Baptist meeting house is 4 miles west of Axminster and about a mile south of Dalwood, off the A35 to Honiton. A small car park is available. The National Trust, who carefully restored it, have cared for it since 1969 and a visit is worthwhile. No charge is made for entry.

The simple thatched building, originally dug into the hillside to avoid attracting attention, was built about 1653 in a secluded spot, surrounded at that time by the dense woodland of Lough Wood. The site was selected because of the official persecution of Baptists at that time, which rose in intensity in the 1680s. According to local legend, its proximity to the border between Devon and Dorset gave the preacher an opportunity to escape to the next county if police were seen approaching during an illegal meeting.

A wheat reed thatched roof covers the gabled building, which has a wire-netted flush ridge with two parallel liggers. A brick chimney protrudes through the west end of the ridge. The National Trust reinstated the thatch to replace a temporary roof of slates. The walls, built mainly of stone rubble, consist of small flints and local stones in a lime

Loughwood Meeting House, Dalwood, Devon

mortar. There are also parts constructed of cob. Buttresses now support the lower gable wall and two others flank the arched entrance door. Alongside the meeting house stands a stone and cob stable, where horses were once fed and watered. This was an essential requirement for both the preacher and congregation, as they travelled long distances to reach the isolated meeting house. The burial ground lies behind on the west side.

Inside the meeting house, wooden steps lead up to the gallery, which is fitted with traditional wooden benches; in the past, musicians would have played stringed instruments there. There are tall box pews made of unvarnished pine on the ground floor. The interior walls are all painted white, as is the plastered barrel vault ceiling. The rounded top windows are all paned with simple clear glass, but leaded. A high octagonal pulpit dominates the east end and the traditional baptismal pool, for total immersion, lies beneath the floorboards in front. Three steps lead down to the water, supplied from a nearby stream. At the west end, below the gallery, there are two small rooms fitted with fireplaces, one of which has a brick floor. They were used to prepare food and keep people warm, who had travelled long distances; one may have been reserved for the women and the other for the men. Above, on the front of the gallery, there is a clock made by John Tratt of Colyton.

Interior of Loughwood Meeting House, Dalwood, Devon

An interesting marble wall tablet pays tribute to Revd Isaac Hann, who served from 1747 to 1778.

> He died in Peace the 17th Day of March
> 1778, Aged 88 years.
> Wit sparkled in his pleasing Face,
> With Zeal his Heart was fir'd;
> Few Ministers so humble were,
> Yet few so much admir'd:
> Ripen'd for Heav'n by Grace divine,
> Like Autumn Fruit he fell;
> Reader think not to live so long,
> But seek to live as well.

He was buried within the confines of the meeting house.

Two framed notices, one on the pulpit and the other by the entrance to the two rear rooms are of historical interest. The one on the pulpit was written by Revd. R. Bastable in 1930.

> Many are the strange and thrilling incidents recorded during the time of persecution. On one occasion when the people were come to the meeting

house they found a Huntsman in the pulpit blowing his horn, and the dogs in the seats. On another Sunday when the people came to worship they found a man standing at the entrance with a drawn sword, with orders to thrust it into the first person who attempted to enter. A dauntless, God-fearing woman, an ancestor of Mr Rippon, of Honiton, was the first who attempted to enter, and with a shriek she forced her way, and others followed, whilst the man stood motionless and like a statue.

Throwleigh – Church of St Mary the Virgin

The church is situated near the centre of the village, which lies about 5 miles south-east of Okehampton. The village is signposted off the A30 Exeter to Okehampton road. The Dartmoor granite church itself is not thatched but it has an unusual thatched lychgate attached to an old thatched church house.

The antiquity of the church house conveys the impression that the lychgate is also old, but it is in fact from the twentieth century. A circular plaque attached to one of the timbers under the thatch of the lychgate reveals that 'it was erected by parishioners and others in memory of George Lincoln Gambien Lowe, Rector 1895–1933'.

Thatched lychgate, St Mary the Virgin, Throwleigh, Devon

A stone pillar on one side supports the timber frame on which the thatch is laid, the other side being supported by the wall of the church house. As is traditional in Devon, combed wheat reed constitutes the material on the roof. Granite stairs from the road lead up to the double gates and there is a granite shelf for resting the bier under the shelter of the thatch. Such shelves were once used whilst awaiting the clergyman's arrival. The churchyard is managed with wild flowers in mind and to the left of the path from the lychgate stands the shaft of an ancient cross, thought probably to date from the fifteenth century.

Uffculme – Spiceland Quaker Meeting House

This meeting house is best reached by leaving the M5 at Junction 27. It lies outside Uffculme, on a minor road at the small hamlet of Prescott. Uffculme itself is situated on the B3440.

The name Spiceland originates from the name of the piece of land on which it was built, with cob and thatch, in 1682. At the same time, a linhay for the horses of those who came to worship was also built of cob and thatch. This original thatched linhay still survives, but it is now used for other purposes. The open-fronted building, with timber supports, has

Linhay at Spiceland Quaker Meeting House, Uffculme, Devon

a wheat reed thatched roof with a plain ridge. The underside of the thatch is exposed and can be seen from inside the linhay. The two small brick buildings at each end represent additions; only the central section retains the original cob walls and thatch. The meeting house itself gradually fell into disrepair and was demolished in 1813. A more substantial seventeenth-century house was rebuilt with a slate roof a few yards away in 1815. The Quakers still meet there in the rear rooms every Sunday at 10.30.

The immaculately kept burial ground behind the meeting house creates an atmosphere of peace and serenity. In the region of 600 people are interred there, many of whom endured long spells of imprisonment and persecution for following their Quaker beliefs. In those early dark days, many Quakers emigrated to America, especially after William Penn, the son of Admiral Sir William Penn, founded the state of Pennsylvania. He had earlier joined the Quakers in England and later drafted the constitution for the state, embodying his liberal political ideas. By coincidence, Pennsylvania came into being in 1682, the same year as the Spiceland Meeting House was opened.

DORSET

Langham – St George's Church

This little thatched church hides away in the tiny settlement of Langham and is difficult to find; road maps rarely mark Langham. It lies towards the edge of the Blackmore Vale, about 2 miles south-west of Gillingham on the minor road leading to Buckhorn Weston. When travelling from Gillingham follow the Wyke road until a signpost indicates a left turn to Buckhorn Weston. St George's is situated a short distance on the left in Langham Lane.

The church was completed in 1921; it is most unusual for one to be built with a thatched roof after the First World War. However, the war became a catalyst for its construction and it was aptly named after St George, the patron saint of soldiers. Alfred Manger, who owned the estate at Langham and lived in Stock Hill House with his wife Elizabeth Ann, laid the initial plans to build a church for the local residents and estate workers on his land. However, war broke out in 1914 before his wish could be fulfilled. Misfortune then struck. His youngest son, Lieutenant J. K. Manger, was killed in action at Ypres in 1915, at the age of twenty-one; his son-in-law, Captain R. Lancaster, and his nephew, George Bredon Kitson, were also killed. He himself died in 1917.

St George, Langham, Dorset

His widow wanted to bring her husband's dream to fruition and approached the Bishop of Salisbury, the Rt Revd Joscelyne. He agreed to consecrate the allocated piece of land and her husband was then buried there. She herself died in 1919 and was also interred there. Later, the rest of the Manger family decided to build the church and employed the architect E. Ponting to design it. He had always admired the thatched church at Freshwater Bay, on the Isle of Wight and designed a simple Arts and Crafts Gothic style church, which was built over the graves of Alfred and Elizabeth. The dedication was conducted on 22 May 1921 by Bishop Joscelyne. The Royal British Legion, which was also established in 1921, held many services there on Remembrance Sunday, but services are now only held at Christmas, Easter and Pentecost. At most other times the church is locked but there is a key-holder whose name can be obtained from the team office at Gillingham and Milton-on-Stour.

St George's stands in an isolated spot in a field with trees close by. The rear of the church is peaceful and looks out over open fields. The combed wheat reed thatched roof has a plain flush ridge. Repairs to the roof first became necessary in 1929 and thirty-three bundles of thatch were used, together with thirty-three bundles of thatching spars. The total cost amounted to about £5. The roof has been repaired and fitted with wire netting several times since, each time at an escalating cost; a rethatch now would cost many thousands of pounds. A small tower with a single bell rises through the ridge at the gabled west end. The bell tower, constructed of wood and louvred slats, supports a small pyramidal roof covered with wood shingles. A small thatched apron below the bell tower adds a finishing touch. At the east end, the church has a rounded apse and the hipped thatch follows the configuration of the stone rubble walls. A small thatched wooden porch on the north side leads into the church. A three-light window, with a small gabled thatch above, is set beside the porch and helps to illuminate the interior.

Inside, several memorials are set in the walls, commemorating various members of the Manger family. One plaque is dedicated to Lieutenant J. K. Manger and his Great War medals are proudly displayed beside it. A barrel roof stands over the central stone aisle below, with a wooden floor laid each side of it. The individual seats are covered with rush. Unusually, there is no font; formerly when a baptism took place a table was brought in and a wooden bowl placed on it.

Tiles protect the floor of the chancel. A small, rounded arched recess, now used as a vestry, branches off the north side of the chancel and is lit by three

Interior of St George, Langham, Dorset

single-light windows. A pair of heavily carved wooden chairs, originally from the Manger house, stand on the south side with the priest's prayer desk between. The wooden lectern displays two bibles belonging to the Manger family. The gravestone in the chancel is that of Alfred Manger and his wife, Elizabeth. The altar rails were donated in memory of Lieutenant Colonel J. Lefroy who became a prisoner of war before Dunkirk in the Second World War. The delightful church stands as a token of remembrance to all those who made the supreme sacrifice during the wars.

ESSEX

DUDDENHOE END – THE HAMLET CHURCH

Duddenhoe End is about 5 miles west of Saffron Walden and 7 miles south-east of Royston. It is signposted off the B1039 on to an unclassified road and after travelling about a mile a further signpost indicates a left turn to the Hamlet Church, one of only two thatched churches in Essex. A stepping-stone path leads to the entrance across a lawn, and the church is left open for visitors. A car park is available.

The Hamlet Church, Duddenhoe End, Essex

Gable end of the Hamlet Church, Duddenhoe End, Essex

A long straw roof shelters the church; a single ligger with spars runs along the eaves level and the north and south gable edges of the thatch. Scallops and points ornament the ridge. It was rethatched in September 1992. A small bell-cote sits on the top of the north gable wall. The walls are constructed of white weatherboarding on a brick base. The adjoining porch is also timber on a brick base and cusps decorate the tops of the openings between the vertical roof supports. A tiled roof with a cross on top protects the structure. The leaded lattice windows of the church vary in shape and size; the small ones in the gable walls are particularly delightful and most unusual. The windows in the south gable wall are new, and the others have been repaired.

The history of the church is interesting, as it was originally built as a tithe barn. The squire parson, the Revd Robert Wilkes of nearby Lofts Hill, organized its conversion into a chapel of ease. It was consecrated on St Peter's Day, 29 June 1859. Local craftsmen carried out the conversion work and the benches were made using timber obtained from the Lofts Hill estate. When St Dunstan's church on the estate was closed, its classical style white marble font and oak communion rail, with its turned balusters, were moved to the Hamlet Church.

By 1990, the church had fallen into a state of disrepair; funds were raised locally and various grants obtained to initiate a renovation. Some of the rotten timbers were replaced, including a section of one of the tie beams. It was during this time that the roof was rethatched, the interior decorated and the porch restored. The church still held services whilst the work was being carried out and its first licence to hold a wedding was granted in 1992. When the renovation was completed, the Bishop of Colchester led a service of rededication on 29 June 1993, the 134th anniversary of the original consecration.

The interior of the church reveals a most unusual arrangement, with the long wall on the east side. This results in the pine benches having to be arranged in long rows in order to face the altar. The benches are divided by three aisles that extend backwards across the short side of the church. These aisles are covered with coconut matting but the rest of the church has exposed wooden floorboards. The benches have open backs, the top rails of which support pine candlesticks with brass tops to hold the candles. Members of the congregation made the needlepoint kneelers, predominantly using aqua-blue and rust-red wool. There are no choir stalls. The area around the font, to the right of the west entrance door, has been left uncluttered and is set aside for children; part is also used as a vestry. All the interior walls, including the sanctuary, are plastered and

Interior of the Hamlet Church, Duddenhoe End, Essex

have wooden panelling to dado height. The lectern is made of pine; there is no pulpit. There is also a wooden arch to the left of the altar by the small electric organ.

The Hamlet Church shares the same grounds as the beautifully thatched church house, which stands a few yards away. It was once occupied by an incumbent but is now a private residence. Open fields surround the buildings. Directly opposite, on the other side of the road, lies the well-kept churchyard; entry is through a tiled lychgate.

Silver End – St Francis

The picturesque thatched St Francis's church stands in Temple Way at Silver End, 4 miles south-east of Braintree and 2 miles north-west of Rivenhall. The church is normally kept locked but several key-holders live nearby. The church was originally a barn, built between 1690 and 1750, and owes its conversion to the creative instincts of F. H. Crittall in the late 1920s. This well-known window manufacturer supplied the metal windows and doors. He also donated the stained glass in 1929. The architect and editor of *The Studio* magazine, Mr. G. C. Holmes, provided the design. When completed the benevolent Crittall family gave the

St Francis, Silver End, Essex

building to the Church of England and it was dedicated to St Francis in September 1930.

In addition to the church, in the late 1920s F. H. Crittall built an entire industrial village on land formerly belonging to Grooms Farm at Silver End to provide housing for employees working at his metal window factory at nearby Braintree, after he expanded his business. The houses were a mixture of brick neo-Georgian and flat-roofed cottages. Shops, a landscaped park and other amenities were also constructed at the same time to make the village self-sufficient. The local authority took over its administration in the 1960s, after the Crittall company was taken over.

The attractive church has weatherboarded walls, and its plain, long perpendicular steel Crittall windows and doors are painted green. The thatch material consists of long straw and the roof was last rethatched in 1988, at a cost of around £10,000. As is usual with a long straw roof, unlike reed, the eaves are ornamented with hazel cross-rods placed between two parallel hazel liggers, all firmly sparred into position for added security. The flush ridge also has decorative cross-rods with a single ligger below. Straw tufts at each end of the ridge complete the rustic appearance.

A large aluminium cross, in the centre of the south wall, hides the position of the original doorway, after it was moved to the extreme left of the building to lead into a south-side porch. The cross was manufactured by the Crittall company in 1968. Two windows each side of it add symmetry to the elevation. A thatched lychgate, also supplied by F. H. Crittall, leads to the church across a large green, where children often play cricket.

All the interior walls are panelled with a light-coloured wood. The wooden theme continues with the font, designed by another member of the Crittall family. The church leaflet states, 'It was hewn from part of an oak tree believed to have been planted near Silver End by King Stephen in the twelfth century – the same year in which St Francis of Assisi was born.' The position of the font is somewhat unusual, as it is near the chancel. As perhaps would be expected, a stained-glass window of St Francis illuminates the church at the east end; the other windows are of plain glass. Originally the church was designed to accommodate 100 parishioners and they sat on individual seats rather than benches. Mr Holmes, the architect who designed the church, also designed the pulpit.

Other interesting features of the church include the tapestries behind the altar and one depicting Leonardo's Last Supper, on the north wall. The church bell came from an old warship and was donated by May and Butcher Ltd of Heybridge, in June 1929. The ceiling of the church was painted a pale blue in 1982, but prior to this a much deeper midnight blue

Chancel of St Francis, Silver End, Essex

had been used, with gold stars. The beams at that time were painted red, with some gold decoration. During the repainting process in 1982, it was discovered that the timber beams were of Scandinavian origin.

HEREFORDSHIRE

Brockhampton – All Saints

This thatched parish church lies about 8 miles from Hereford and 7 miles from Ross-on-Wye off the B4224. It is truly an extraordinary church.

A Grade I listed building, it was built in 1901–2, the gift of Mrs Alice Madeline Foster as a memorial to her parents, Ebenezer D. and Julia Jordan from Boston, Massachusetts, USA. Brockhampton Court, which lies opposite the church, had been purchased by Ebenezer Jordan in the 1870s as a wedding present for Alice when she married Mr Arthur Foster.

Alice Foster commissioned architect W. R. Lethaby to design and supervise the building of All Saints as a replacement for the medieval Church of the Holy Trinity that stood in Brockhampton Court. Lethaby played a leading part in the creation of the School of Arts and Crafts and

All Saints, Brockhampton, Herefordshire

was a disciple of William Morris. Lethaby placed much emphasis on the quality and variety of the materials used for the building of the church and also the vernacular craftsmanship, incorporating as many local materials as possible. The walls were constructed from Herefordshire stone and the supporting triangular buttresses complement the walls and the rest of the building because of their texture and unusual shape. The buttresses are capped with lead. Unfortunately, several structural errors were made in the construction and many other problems were encountered that escalated the costs. This seemed to affect Lethaby's confidence and he retired from his architectural practice shortly afterwards, refusing even his fee. Despite this, he left us with a truly remarkable, most unusual and impressive early twentieth-century church, built in the medieval style.

The church, sloping from west to east, has been rethatched several times, most recently in 2000. A mixture of Norfolk and French water reed was chosen as the thatch material. A raised ridge, decorated with points, was used over the chancel end and below it two raised thatched aprons were made, one ornamented with scallops and points and the other, just above the eaves level, with semicircles. In contrast, to the left of the central stone tower, over the nave end, the thatched roof ridge was left plain with a straight raised ridge. To harmonize with the thatch decorations, the top of the central tower was ornamented with pointed stone chevrons.

Horizontal oak weatherboarding clads the bell tower, which stands over the south entrance porch of the church. Its top is capped by a pyramidal roof cloaked with cedar wood shingles. There are two bells in the tower and the larger one, according to the church leaflet, bears an inscription: 'Not in words but with my voice will I sing praises to my Lord.'

Natural stone and oak feature highly throughout the church, including the porch and short transepts. The impressive steep transverse arches in the nave are fashioned from a local sandstone, as are the window spaces. One of the windows commemorates Alice Foster's sister, Julia. The vaulting consists of concrete but it is not reinforced, probably because it supports only a thatched roof, which is much lighter than a more conventional tile or slate roof. The porch, with its impressive double-entry doors made of oak with ornamented wrought iron hinges, is interesting, as is the rounded inner door leading into the nave. Above this door are, six doves of peace, carved in stone, with a carved panel above displaying a cross and stars.

Many of the beautiful stained-glass windows in the church are by Christopher Whall, including the striking east window with its six-pointed star over the three lancets below, which show seven saints and two angels. Whall was noted for the quality of his stained-glass work; the best example of his craftsmanship may be seen in the Chapter House of

Interior arches in All Saints, Brockhampton, Herefordshire

Gloucester Cathedral. Lethaby designed the circular stone font, with its beautifully carved bowl decorated with two interwoven friezes of grape vines. Members of the Foster family donated it in memory of their grandparents. The pulpit, constructed of oak, has a carved panel of Christ preaching to country people whilst their children play happily nearby.

The Ancient and Modern hymnals are another unusual feature. They have linen covers, hand-embroidered with a wide variety of wild flowers. The seat cushions also display wild flower needlework. The theme continues in the chancel, where the forty-eight inset panels on the front of the oak choir stalls were carved with wild flowers by George Jack, a noted wood carver. The original altar cloth also follows the floral theme but has now been removed for preservation. However, it can still be seen displayed in a glass cabinet on the west wall of the church. The seat covers, hymnal flower covers and altar cloth were all given by an anonymous lady donor in 1960 as a tribute to the wild flowers carved on the choir stalls and in an appreciation of the fact that the church was left open to visitors. She also donated a hand-written book, in which she described all the wild flowers depicted in the church and found in the churchyard.

The reredos shows a fifteenth-century Italian relief depicting the Virgin and Child and a female saint, possibly St Anne. Two tapestries of angels, made in the workshops of William Morris from a design by Edward Burne-Jones, are on either side of the altar. The original design was created for a stained-glass window in Salisbury Cathedral in 1875.

Another treasure to be found in the church is a sixteenth-century triptych displayed in a wall cabinet opposite the original altar cloth on the west wall. The main central panel shows the Crucifixion, with St John the Baptist in a small semicircular panel above; six other small panels depict other scenes, including Christ in the Temple, before Herod and being scourged. The two wings of the triptych are Flemish; the left one pictures Jesus with the three Marys and the right one Jesus being lowered from the cross. Nearby may be found the ceremonial mallet used by Alice Foster when she laid the foundation stone of the church on 21 June 1901.

Finally, the Grade 2 listed lychgate that leads into the churchyard has massive semicircular stone supports for its hipped thatched roof, furnished with a rich deep straight ridge. The entry gates are made of oak. The churchyard is well kept and many wild flowers thrive to encourage wildlife. Just inside the lychgate stands a war memorial, in honour of those who gave their lives during the two world wars.

Thatched lychgate at All Saints, Brockhampton, Herefordshire

ISLE OF WIGHT

Freshwater Bay – St Agnes

The thatched church of St Agnes stands in Gate Lane, opposite the post office at Freshwater Bay, on the south-west side of the island. The A3055 leads to it from the village of Freshwater. Lord Tennyson, son of the Poet Laureate, donated the land on which it was built in 1908. The Bishop of Winchester officiated at the dedication in the same year, before the roof was completed. Lord Tennyson lived nearby at Farringford, which was originally purchased by Alfred, Lord Tennyson from the proceeds of his poem Maud. St Agnes replaced the building where services were formerly held, locally known as the Iron Room, in the Square. The need for a new church arose because the villagers complained that the Iron Room was too cold in winter and too hot in summer, as well as looking uninviting. The new church, with its thatched roof, was by contrast, warm in the winter, cool in the summer and an attractive building.

Lady Tennyson suggested the dedication to St Agnes, the virgin martyr of Rome, whom she much admired for her courage and devotion.

St Agnes, Freshwater Bay, Isle of Wight

She had refused to marry when only a girl of thirteen because of her dedication to Christ. For this and her refusal to deny her Christian faith, the Romans put her to the sword by piercing her throat, probably around AD 305. It is thought likely she died on 21 January, the date celebrated in the Christian calendar as St Agnes Day.

The church is the only one with a thatched roof on the Isle of Wight and interestingly, is the first building on the island to be thatched with Norfolk reed. It is now a listed building. The architect Isaac Jones of Herne Hill, London, designed it and based his plans on a water-colour painted by the Rector of Freshwater at that time, the Revd A. J. Robertson. He completed the painting to give the architect an impression of the type of church he envisaged.

The original Norfolk reed roof, which was done by a Norwich thatcher, gave excellent long service and it was not until 1962 that a rethatch became necessary. This was carried out again using Norfolk reed at a cost of £600. Unfortunately, extensive repairs became necessary in 1979 and the cost rose to £9,000. Scallops and points ornament the ridge; this is common with a Norfolk reed roof. It is widely found throughout East Anglia. The thatched eaves undulate attractively, in gabled and half-hipped form, over the stone windows. Two tiny blocked windows on the south side also quaintly peep through the main body of the thatch. One end of the church is gabled and the other hipped. A small bell-cote with a cross tops the roof and contains a single bell. It is pyramidal, with wooden slats, and is roofed with red tiles obtained from an old derelict farmhouse, close by at Hooke Hill. Robert Hooke the famous seventeenth-century scientist, who postulated the law of elasticity known as Hooke's Law, once lived there. Lady Tennyson donated the north porch of St Agnes as a memorial to her mother; it has similar tiles on its gabled roof.

Most of the building stone used in the construction of the church also came from the farmhouse. This gives the church an aged appearance. One large stone, incised with the date 1694, may be found near the outside vestry door. It came from the barn of the old farmhouse. However, the stone confuses many visitors, giving the false impression that the church dates from the seventeenth century rather than from the Edwardian period.

The inside of the church reveals a unique wooden chancel screen carved with grapes and vines to depict the eucharist and lilies for purity. The Revd Thomas Gardner Devitt carved it during his period as curate of the parish in the 1940s. He also carved it richly with other Christian symbols. It is thought likely that he also carved the Lamb of God on the front of the altar, the altar rails and the poppyhead choir stalls.

Interior of St Agnes, Freshwater Bay, Isle of Wight

The Latin inscription on the left side of the altar rail reads '*AGNUS DEI QUI TOLLIS*' and to the right '*PECCATA MUNDI MISERERE NOBIS*', which translates as 'Lamb of God, who takes away the sins of the world, have mercy upon us.' The left-hand base of the chancel screen has 'This is the House Of God' and the right 'This is the Gate of Heaven.'

Several plaques adorn the interior walls, in memory of those who had held strong associations with the church. The north wall has one to the god-daughter of the Poet Laureate, whilst the south wall pays tribute to the memory of the architect who designed the church, Isaac Jones. Another tablet remembers Anne-Isabella Ritchie, the daughter of the writer William Makepeace Thackeray. Both the ceiling and the floor are constructed of wood and individual chairs line each side of the single aisle. All the arched windows are of clear glass and mainly arranged in groups of two or three. There is no east window in the apsidal wall of the sanctuary but there are two single windows at each side of the altar.

A large beautifully carved wooden chest stands against the east wall. It came from the former garrison church of St Andrew, Norton, which was used by service personnel during the Second World War. Finally, the original wooden organ remains in the church and the lever handle by which it was formerly pumped may still be seen, despite the fact that it now operates by electricity.

LINCOLNSHIRE

Markby – St Peter

Markby village lies on the A1111, about 2 miles north-east of the market town of Alford, and claims the only remaining thatched church in Lincolnshire. St Peter's stands on the site of the former twelfth-century Markby Priory, founded by the Augustinian Canons. Parts of the masonry from the ruins are incorporated into the church's structure. It was probably rebuilt in 1611 and includes a dated beam salvaged from Markby Priory. The moat that surrounded the priory still remains around the church.

Separate reed thatched roofs cover the nave and chancel, which is lower. Points decorate the nave ridge, but only one central point ornaments the small chancel ridge. A little window sheltered by a canopy of thatch peeps through the south slope of the nave roof. Crosses stand on the top of the west and east gable stone walls, both of which are buttressed.

The south doorway has a pointed arch, whilst the northern older one is round-arched. Folklore relates that if a person runs around the church three times at midnight and then hammers a nail into the church door, he or she will see a ghost. Hundreds of nails have been hammered into the old door in an attempt to encourage the apparition to put in an appearance. All the windows were inserted in the seventeenth century. Those in the nave are of three lights, with the exception of one in the west wall, and those in the chancel are of two lights, including the east window.

The interior contains an octagonal font from an earlier church standing on the tiled floor of the nave. The stem is also octagonal but the cover is round. A mixture of original benches and box pews has survived, as well as a rare two-decker pulpit. A wooden chest may also be seen, which was possibly constructed from ancient oak beams salvaged from Markby Priory. The chancel arch contains some thirteenth-century dogtooth ornamentation that probably also came from the priory and was inserted when St Peter's was rebuilt in 1611. The communion rail is three-sided and the plain altar table sits on pillar supports.

NORFOLK

Acle – St Edmund

Acle's location just off the A47, to the east of Norwich, makes it a popular base for touring the Broads. The thatched St Edmund's church may be found in Norwich Road, near the centre of the village.

It is thought that the Saxons built its flint round tower and that the octagonal top was added later, in the thirteenth century. The battlements were built on top in the fifteenth century, with eight statues added as pinnacles in each corner of the octagon. The one on the south-east corner is of St Edmund. There is a modern clock on the tower and within it there are six bells.

A reed thatched roof shelters the large nave and points decorate its ridge. A slate roof covers the chancel and a leaded roof protects the two-storeyed north porch that leads into the church. The porch, constructed of knapped flints, dates from the late fifteenth century; its arch has two small windows above. There is also a two-storeyed south porch that was the original entrance, with a scratch dial on its wall and a sturdy oak door. Both nave and chancel mainly date to the fourteenth century but a few parts are Norman. The walls consist chiefly of flint rubble.

St Edmund, Acle, Norfolk

St Edmund's font, Acle, Norfolk

On entry into the church, the impressive lofty font cover immediately attracts attention. The octagonal stone font has the date 1410 on its top pedestal but its towering wooden cover is modern, having been donated in 1933. Carved images of lions and 'wodewoses' alternate around the font's stem; wodewoses are wild, hairy, bearded men bearing clubs. They appear frequently on fifteenth-century fonts with lions, which in mythology they could catch and control. They began as demons guarding woods but became confused with hairy satyrs. Later, living in woods away from worldly sin they became symbols of a pure life. Several carved symbols decorate the bowl, including the trinity, the pietà (the Virgin Mary holding Christ's dead body on her lap), the four evangelists and angels. Some of the images retain traces of their original colouring but several of the faces were vandalized during the Commonwealth period and later restored.

The south door has a gallery above it and the Ten Commandments are written each side. The plain benches in the nave are hollow-backed but some of the choir stalls have poppyhead ends. Most of the leaded light windows are of clear glass but there is a Victorian stained-glass east window showing the ascension and another in the north wall behind the pulpit. A barrel-vaulted wooden roof covers the nave and a wooden slatted scissor-brace roof towers over the chancel. The floors consist of wood and tiles. The coat of arms reads '*Dieu et mon droit*'.

A striking feature in the chancel is an inscription written in charcoal on the plaster of the north wall behind the choir stall. It was uncovered in 1912 and stabilized. Expert opinion suggests it was written in the fifteenth century, when there were still some outbreaks of the Black Death occurring throughout the country. Although written in Latin, the church has helpfully provided an acceptable translation beside it. It reads:

O lamentable Death, how many dost thou cast in the pit
Anon the infants fade away, and of the aged death makes an end.
Now these, now those thou ravagest, O Death on every side.
These that wear horn [headdresses] or veils, fate spareth not
Therefore while in the world the brute beast, plague rages hour by hour
With prayer and with remembrance deplore death's deadliness.

Interestingly, the women of East Anglia wore hats made from horn at the time of the plague.

The lovely painted fifteenth-century wooden rood screen has intricate tracery and rises high towards the top of the chancel arch. It is not the original screen but is thought to have come from an abbey or priory. One

St Edmund's rood screen, Acle, Norfolk

of the motifs on the base shows the letter E, with the crossed arrows that symbolize St Edmund. The rood on the top of the screen was added much later, in 1939. The opening for the rood loft still survives high on the south wall; originally there was access from an outside door on the north wall, where a stained-glass window has been inserted. To the right of the chancel arch there is a lovely painted panel on the wall, behind an altar dedicated to Our Lady. It shows a central figure, with a bishop's crook and a book with separate green-patterned material panels on each side. Also to the right of the chancel arch there is a niche. A piscina may be found on the south wall of the sanctuary.

Babingley – St Felix Chapel

Her Majesty the Queen owns the thatched St Felix Chapel, which stands on the Royal Sandringham Estate. Babingley lies north of King's Lynn and may be reached off the A149. There is parking on site and railings surround the churchyard.

In 1894–5, the Prince of Wales, later to become King Edward VII, built a corrugated iron church, manufactured by Boulton and Paul of Norwich, to replace the nearby medieval church of St Felix, which had fallen into a ruinous state. It was fairly common at that time to buy special kits. There were several manufacturers who marketed them and carried out the construction work. Various sizes were available. The new church was given a Norfolk reed thatched roof and the interior lined with American pine panelling. The Church of England worshipped there until 1980, when it was declared redundant and the royal estate resumed ownership.

During the following twenty years it gradually fell into a state of disrepair, although it had occasional use as a youth centre. The stained-glass windows suffered damage during its period of idleness. Fortunately, despite the distressed look of the thatched roof, it still managed to keep the interior dry and sound. In May 2000, the Queen offered the gift of the lease to the British Orthodox Church, in return for them maintaining the building and its churchyard, which had become very overgrown. Earlier negotiations had taken place in 1988.

The Orthodox community moved in during May and began regular Sunday worship. Work began in earnest during October to restore the church to its former charming exterior appearance. The total cost amounted to £30,000; the congregation provided the majority of the money and the Norfolk Churches Trust donated £10,000. The chapel now serves the British Orthodox parish of St Mary and St Felix, which includes West Norfolk and King's Lynn. It is part of the Coptic Orthodox Patriarchate of Alexandria, Egypt, one of the most ancient Orthodox churches, founded in Alexandria by St Mark the Evangelist in AD 58. Orthodox Christians remain faithful to the unchanging truths of the gospels of Christ revealed by the apostles.

The Norfolk reed roof that shelters the chapel has a scalloped ridge, with tiny triangular windows peeping through the thatch just below the ridge, with small ornamented thatched aprons below. The main thatched roof sweeps out effortlessly from the main slope to cover the two arched entrances, built at right angles to the main building. Crosses perch on the end gable walls. The windows have Y-tracery, with crossbars below. Repairs to the fabric of the chapel started in 2005 and will continue over a five-year period.

The chapel was aptly dedicated to St Felix, as it lies about ½ mile from where the patron saint started his ministry in Britain; the site is marked where the old St Felix church now stands as a ruin. St Felix was born in Burgundy in about 595, and later joined a monastery. He became acquainted with Prince Sigebert, who had been exiled from East Anglia, and Felix converted him to the Christian faith. Later, Prince Sigebert returned to East Anglia to be crowned as king. He invited St Felix to leave France and preach in his kingdom, in order to convert his heathen subjects. First, Felix went to Canterbury to receive Archbishop Honorius's blessing for his evangelizing task and then sailed up the coast into the Wash and along the Babingley River to found what was probably the first Christian church in Norfolk. He also set about missionary work all over East Anglia. The feast day of St Felix is celebrated on 8 March. The chapel holds divine liturgy each Sunday at 10.30.

Bacton – St Andrew

Bacton is situated close to the coast and near the massive North Sea gas terminal. It is north-east of North Walsham off the A149 Cromer to Great Yarmouth road. St Andrew's stands just outside the village to the west, in an isolated churchyard. There is ample space for car parking and the church is open during the day. It consists of a fifteenth-century square tower that ascends in five separate stages of decreasing sizes, a nave and a thatched chancel. Battlements top the flint tower, with a weather-vane on top. Both chancel and nave also date from the fifteenth century and their walls are built of squared flint and freestone. Buttresses support the walls.

The chancel was rethatched in 2004/5 at a cost of £27,000; despite Norfolk being the home of the famous Norfolk reed, the thatch material

St Andrew, Bacton, Norfolk

used was Egyptian water reed – a strange decision but probably made on grounds of cost and availability. Some 1,400 bundles of reed were needed. Scallops and points provide the decoration for the ridge. Tiles now cover the nave roof but in 1823 it was cloaked with lead. Both nave and chancel gable walls have a cross on top. The south porch has a slate roof, with a blue statue of St Francis in a niche above the semicircular arch of the door. It is made of pottery and replaced the original statue of the saint, which was stolen; the thief needed a ladder to reach it. The south doorway leading into the church has mouldings around it. The leaded-light windows have tracery, with a mixture of clear and stained glass. The nave has two stained-glass windows, whilst the chancel contains three, including the large three-light window in the east wall. They are all Victorian.

The Victorians carried out a major internal restoration in 1895. However, the original octagonal fifteenth-century font still remains. It stands on a raised platform and the bowl displays the winged symbols of the four evangelists, St Matthew's man, St Mark's lion, St Luke's ox and St John's eagle, together with four angels bearing shields. Carved animals decorate the base. The font has an elaborate wooden cover on top, furnished with a tall, rounded finial. The timbers of the chancel ceiling are pale blue and flower bosses adorn them. The nave ceiling is timbered. The piscina displays the remains of aged paint. A large ancient stone statue of a figure in a truncated

St Andrew's pews, Bacton, Norfolk

form stands in front and it is thought it might have originally been a decorative piece removed from the tower. There are tiles behind the altar.

The pews on each side of the single aisle are varied and somewhat unusual; they are all fitted with brass handles at their ends. These are used for the storage of umbrellas; one lifts the handles, inserts the umbrellas and places the points in the drip trays below. All the pews are numbered and a few at the west end have poppyheads. The choir stalls all have poppyhead finials. The hassocks or kneelers, on the pew prayer book rests are of a large variety of designs, including St Peter's cross keys as a symbol of the Church's authority, fleurs-de-lis and other flower varieties.

The ruins of Bacton Abbey, known locally as Bromholm Priory, may be found nearby. It was also dedicated to St Andrew and became famous as a place of pilgrimage because of its possession of a 'true relic of the Holy Cross'.

Barton Bendish – St Mary

Barton Bendish is about halfway between Downham Market and Swaffham and may be reached off the A1122. St Mary's is a picturesque little church that lies on the western outskirts of the tiny village, in a quiet

St Mary, Barton Bendish, Norfolk

location surrounded by trees. A key-holder lives nearby. The fourteenth-century thatched church became redundant in 1974 and the Churches Conservation Trust has cared for it since 1976. It is mainly constructed of flint and rubble, with some lime rendering. A Norfolk reed thatched roof covers the nave and chancel, with a small parapet wall dividing the two surfaces. Scallops ornament the ridge. The former south porch was converted into a vestry in 1789 and this has a thatched roof with a straight, unadorned ridge. The Victorians may have later rebuilt the vestry.

A striking feature for Norfolk is the absence of a west tower. It fell down during a severe storm in 1710, destroying the west end of the nave. Neither was rebuilt; in 1789 the damaged nave west end was repaired but left in its shortened form. However, a magnificent Norman doorway, salvaged from the demolished All Saints church nearby was inserted in the rebuilt west wall. This now gives entry to the church. The outside semicircle of its arch, serving as a hood-mould, has dogtooth carvings, the middle circle beakhead motifs and the inner circle arch bobbin mouldings. The shafts below have leaf-like carvings and bobbins. A cupola was erected at the west end of the nave roof in 1789 to house a bell but this was replaced in 1871 by a bell-cote with a cross on top, containing one bell of

Norman doorway at St Mary, Barton Bendish, Norfolk

1691. Another cross perches on the top of the east gable wall. There is a small priest's door on the south side of the chancel, with a crocketed ogee arch. Nearly all the windows have fourteenth-century tracery.

The interior is simple, with a single tiled aisle and whitewashed walls. The two-light Victorian west window shows Christ healing the sick and blessing little children. A large, faded fourteenth-century wall painting survives on the south nave wall. It depicts a female figure, a large wheel and a two-handled bier below. The figure may be St Catherine of Alexandria who was tortured on a wheel. However, the wheel has many other symbolic interpretations and the fact that it is shown with a bier casts some doubt whether the figure depicts St Catherine. An interesting mix of box pews and benches provide the seating. The former date from 1789 but the Victorians cut them to a smaller size in 1865. One of the plain benches at the rear is incised with the date 1637.

The font has a hexagonal bowl, with fourteenth-century-style carvings and was donated in 1857. The chancel has an altar table dated 1633, a medieval aumbry and a sedilia in the south wall, with its front decorated with quatrefoils. There are memorial slabs in the sanctuary floor and various memorial tablets on the walls.

Beachamwell – St Mary the Virgin

Beachamwell is situated about 5 miles south-west of Swaffham and may be reached off either the A1122 or the A1065. St Mary the Virgin church dates to Saxon times and both its nave and chancel are thatched with water reed. Points decorate the ridges, with neat thatch aprons below terminating in inverted scallops on the north side.

The beautiful church possesses an unusual highly decorated flint tower. The round section dates from the tenth century but the octagonal belfry stage was added in the fourteenth. The higher part of the Saxon round section has four two-light window openings, two facing south and east with arched heads, two to the north and west with triangular heads. Below these, small lancet windows peep out to the west and south. The upper octagonal stage of the tower has four double belfry openings with tracery, alternating around the tower faces with matching tracery patterns of knapped flint and dressed stone. A slim lead spike perches on top of the roof, with a weather-vane. The belfry contains two bells that are thought to be of the fifteenth century.

A low buttressed south aisle of knapped flint was added to the nave during the fourteenth century and its leaded roof fits snugly below the

St Mary the Virgin, Beachamwell, Norfolk

eaves of the thatch. The remains of two medieval scratch dials are carved on its south doorway. The exterior north wall of the nave is interesting because large parts of it may be Saxon, as indicated by the long-and-short work of the quoins to the west. The north porch has an attractive brick crow-stepped gable, added in the fifteenth or sixteenth century. Tiles cover the roof and the brick walls are rendered. Most of the leaded-light windows in the church are of the fifteenth century and filled with clear glass. The exceptions are the Victorian stained-glass east window and the south aisle east window of 1903. Both are traceried three-lights.

The interior of the church contains a south arcade of four bays, with some rare graffiti carved by a medieval mason on the south-west piers, recording a list of the various building materials used for the construction of the arcade, together with the quantities. Nearby, there is a grotesque carving of the Devil with his tongue protruding and a stick raised in his left hand, no doubt ready to beat the souls in Hell. Through the arcade, the south aisle contains an altar for use as a lady chapel. There is also a piscina halfway down the aisle, the niche of which now shelters a statue of the Virgin Mary. The position of the piscina indicates that the east end of the arcade bays was a later extension.

There are several commemorative plaques on the aisle wall, including three to long serving churchwardens. At the east end of the aisle is an unusual chest supported on legs designed by John Matthew, lord of the manor. It was made by the famous London lock-makers, Joseph Bramah and Son. The chest was constructed in 1835; fine iron fretwork ornaments each side and there are also octagonal shafts. It was originally designed for dual use as an altar and parish chest. The stained glass east window of the aisle depicts our Lord healing the sick.

A mixture of hexagonal tiles and local bricks provides an attractive floor. The benches are all Victorian and have poppyhead ends. The pulpit and reader's desk are Jacobean and stand in the chancel, in front of an elaborate blocked fifteenth-century arch that formerly led to the vestry. The chancel has two interesting monument brasses in the floor. One shows the full-length fourteenth-century figure of a priest, beautifully dressed in his vestments, the other a demi-figure of the Revd John Grymestone, who died in 1430 and was rector for five years. The altar came from the redundant nearby tiny church of St Botolph at Shingham.

Beighton – All Saints

Beighton lies about 8 miles east of Norwich and may be reached via the A47 and B1140. The church is signposted off the latter and lies in Church Hill. It is normally locked.

All Saints, Beighton, Norfolk

The nave of the fourteenth-century church is reed thatched, with a straight ridge. The thatched eaves undulate in 'eyebrows' over the three two-light clerestory windows that look out over the slated south aisle roof. The south porch, which leads into the aisle, also has a slate roof, as do the north aisle and chancel. Buttresses support the aisle walls, which are mainly constructed of flint, as is the short, square west tower. The lower part of the tower dates to the fourteenth century but the upper section, with an embattled top, was added in the late nineteenth century. A statue of a saint stands at each corner of the parapet and the lower part of the tower has a stained-glass west window. As well as the south door, the church also has a priest's door of the fourteenth century.

The windows in the aisles mainly have Y-tracery with Victorian glass. The octagonal font dates from the thirteenth century and its panels are ornamented with thinly recessed pointed arches. Both arcades consist of four bays with octagonal piers supporting the arches. The benches are decorated with various animal carvings on their ends. Parts of the chancel screen date from the fifteenth century, the sedilia has ogee arches and crockets. A small flint-built vestry lies off the north wall of the chancel.

The church was once the guardian of a rare early seventeenth-century chest, made of yew and ornamented. The lid contained an image of Susanna and the Elders, who tried in vain to seduce her by making false accusations against her. In Christian art, she became a symbol of purity and the triumph of a righteous person over evil. The chest was removed to the St Peter Hungate Church Museum in Princes Street, Norwich, for safekeeping.

Billockby – All Saints

Billockby is situated 2 miles north-east of Acle and lies by the A1064. All Saints church stands in an isolated position. Disaster struck it on 15 July 1762, when a violent storm raged and lightning struck its tower. The flint top section fell onto the nave, causing widespread damage, not only to the building but also to the interior furnishings including the benches, pulpit and reader's desk. The shattered nave was never rebuilt and the picturesque ruins still remain, together with those of the tower, which has huge vertical cracks stretching from top to bottom.

The flint chancel survived large-scale damage and services continued; however, extensive renovation did not take place until 1872. It is still in use and a reed thatch with a straight ridge shelters its scissor-braced roof.

The windows have Y-tracery, except for the large three-light east window, which has intersecting tracery. Buttresses support the corners of the east wall. The doorway leading into the chancel has a pointed arch. The Perpendicular octagonal font, probably rescued from the ruined nave, has plain panels on its bowl, with traceried ones on the stem.

The original south porch of knapped flint, which leads into the ruins of the nave, has since been restored and a thatched roof shelters it; a single central scallop decorates the otherwise straight ridge. The porch entrance has a statue niche above its moulded pointed arch. The gaunt ruin of the nave behind still retains its large empty Perpendicular window spaces and buttressed walls.

Brumstead – St Peter

The village is situated near East Ruston, off the B1159 to the north of the A149, at Stalham. A continuous reed thatched roof flows over the nave and chancel of St Peter's and its south porch is also thatched. Scallops and points decorate the ridges of both.

The church records reveal that St Peter's was given a new roof in 1834, when its nave roof was at two different levels and in disrepair. A continuous level roof was constructed and thatched with water reed at a cost of £200. The roof received further attention when restoration of the church took place in 1867. It has obviously been rethatched several times since, the latest in the 1990s. An inspection in 1993 revealed that the thatch had suffered considerable damage and even parts of the rafters were exposed by the thatch slipping; the metal rods and iron hooks fixing the thatch to the roof timbers were also partly visible. The porch thatch was also severely damaged by rainwater cascading on to it from the south roof slope of the nave. After the roofs were rethatched, a rainwater gutter was fixed along the eaves of the south nave to prevent a recurrence.

The church dates back to the late fourteenth and early fifteenth centuries. The flint west tower has diagonal buttresses at the corners and a west doorway, with a small stained-glass window above. The sound holes in the belfry are in quatrefoil form, with louvred openings below. The tower is embattled and grotesque carved gargoyles at the corners throw rainwater clear of its roof. The belfry now only houses one bell, cast in about 1470; at one time there were three but two were sold to raise funds for the church in the early eighteenth century.

Two types of buttress support the flint cobbled walls of the church.

St Peter, Brumstead, Norfolk

Some are of flint and stone, whilst others are of brick, probably of a later date. Most of the windows on the south side of the nave have cusped intersecting tracery and are fitted with clear glass. The stained-glass east window, inserted in 1875, has the same type of tracery. The windows in the north wall also have tracery but are not cusped; they are fitted with clear glass.

The thatched porch leading into the church has a niche above the arch but with the statue missing; it once contained one of St Peter, to whom the church is dedicated. The south doorway into the church has a moulded arch and probably dates from the fourteenth century. There is also a similar blocked north doorway, with a tablet above recording that the roof was renewed in 1834. The door leading into the tower from the church is the original, dating from when the church was first built. St Peter's is single-celled.

The Victorians installed pews with poppyhead ends. The fourteenth-century octagonal font displays quatrefoil decoration on the bowl and the stem is panelled. The Victorians provided the pulpit and the reading desk. The entrance to the stairs that led up to the former rood loft still survives in the south wall. The piscina in the sanctuary dates to the fifteenth century but the Ten Commandments and the Creed featured each side of the altar are Victorian.

BURGH-NEXT-AYLSHAM – ST MARY

The village stands about 10 miles north of Norwich and may be reached off the A140 to the east of Aylsham. The churchyard of St Mary's stretches down to the picturesque banks of the River Bure. It contains some unusual simple wooden crosses along the outside east wall of the church. A small pitched roof shields each cross. They are grave markers and two of them remember the Revd Thomas Barnes and his son, who were both rectors of the church and died during the First World War.

A thatched roof covers the chancel and scallops decorate the ridge. It was rethatched in 1981. The nave roof is tiled, although it was thatched until 1903, when a new scissor-beam roof, covered with Broseley tiles, replaced it. At the same time, a new north porch was built. The Perpendicular square west tower is embattled and faced with knapped flints. Buttresses support each corner of the structure. The sound holes have tracery and the belfry contains a single bell. Although sound holes are primarily designed to allow the ringing bells to be heard, they also fulfil the equally important function of allowing light and air into the ringing chamber. The nave and chancel walls are constructed of knapped flints and attractive ornamented buttresses of stone and flint support them. The church basically dates to the early thirteenth century but has undergone many alterations.

Grave markers at St Mary, Burgh-next-Aylsham, Norfolk

St Mary, Burgh-next-Aylsham, Norfolk

The Victorians were responsible for a particularly heavy restoration of the nave but a more artistic one of the chancel. The octagonal fifteenth-century font, ornamented with statuettes and shields on the stem, survives. The outer panels of the bowl are carved with images depicting the seven sacraments: baptism, communion, confirmation, penance or confession, extreme unction or the Catholic last rites, holy orders and matrimony. Protestants generally only recognize the first two, but Catholics recognize all seven. Of course, when the font was made all churches in England were of the Catholic faith.

The leaded-light windows with Y-tracery in the nave are of clear glass, which has the effect of making the interior very light. Quarry tiles cover the nave floor and the pews have foliage decoration on the prayer-book slopes. The beautiful pictorial kneelers show a variety of Norfolk scenes. An eighteenth-century copy of *The Adoration of the Magi* by Gentile da Fabriano hangs on the west wall. The original, painted in 1423, now hangs in the Uffizi in Florence. On the north and south walls, the stations of the cross are displayed in frames.

Unusually, two steps lead down rather than up into the wide impressive chancel with its glorious arcading. The roof is in the simple trussed rafter form that was fashionable in the thirteenth century. It now has added semicircular arched braces. An elaborate arch on the north side

Chancel arcading at St Mary, Burgh-next-Aylsham, Norfolk

gives access to a small north chapel that was rebuilt in 1876–8. It contains the only stained glass in the church, in lancet windows showing six Christian motifs and emblems. At the same date, the chancel was extended eastwards and extra lancet windows added. The east wall has a tall three-light Perpendicular window, with a separate small round window above. A plaque in the chancel states that the renovations and extensions were done 'To the Glory of God and in Honour of the Blessed Virgin Mary'. The Victorian church architect Richard M. Phipson was responsible for them, after consultation with Sir George Gilbert Scott, the famous architect, designer and restorer of medieval buildings. Terracotta tiles cover the chancel floor.

Burgh St Margaret – St Margaret

Burgh St Margaret is situated about 6 miles north-west of Great Yarmouth overlooking the nearby marshland. The church is kept locked, but a churchwarden can be contacted for viewing. It has a thatched nave and chancel, both with straight ridges, and a parapet wall separates the two roof surfaces; the chancel stands at a lower level than the nave. A curious three-light dormer window, with a thatched canopy flowing over it, has been built in the west end slope of the nave roof, directly over the south porch; old prints of the church show that it was not there in the early nineteenth century. It snuggles very close to the square west tower.

The church underwent extensive restoration in 1876, when the roofs were replaced. Unfortunately, a fire broke out in 1898 and the roof had to be rebuilt again. The fire destroyed all the early parish records. It was after the fire that the unusual thatched dormer was constructed. The window was added to light an open-fronted gallery that was built at the same time, with a steep twisting flight of stairs giving access to it. The gallery was fitted with several tiered rows of pews, but these were removed in 1990 to convert it into a meeting room and crèche. Windows were installed in the open front to overlook the nave.

The west tower of flint and rubble is unbuttressed and the embattlements were added in 1900. The arched louvred bell openings below have Y-tracery. The tower houses three bells; since 1990 they have been rung with shortened bell ropes from a new room constructed over the vestry. Previously, they were rung from the vestry itself, in the base of the tower. The church has two Norman doorways, the south one with zigzag and billet carvings in the arch, the north with only billet ornamentation. Buttresses support both the nave and chancel walls and most of the Perpendicular-style traceried windows are Victorian replacements. There is a single row of red brick ornamentation over their stone hood-moulds.

The font and chancel arch both formed part of the 1876 restoration. The south chancel wall bears an interesting small brass, picturing a figure of John Burton, who was rector for twenty-eight years and died in 1608. He is depicted kneeling at a prayer desk, dressed in ruff and gown. There is also a more modern inscription to the Rt Revd George Carnac Fisher, Bishop of Ipswich and incumbent 1898–1921.

Burgh St Peter – St Mary

Burgh St Peter lies about 5 miles west of Lowestoft and 3 miles north-east of Beccles and may be reached off the A143. St Mary's church is located by the River Waveney, about a mile outside the village. A continuous reed thatched roof sweeps over the nave and the chancel, and a separate thatch shelters the south porch. The ridges have points and below them deep thatch aprons terminate with inverted scallops, just above the eaves level. The roof was rethatched in 1998, after a fire caused considerable damage.

The bizarre stepped west tower, erected as a mausoleum for members of the Revd Samuel Boycott's family, constitutes the most unusual feature of the church. It was built in 1793. Generations of the Boycott family once served as rectors to the church. An exception was Charles Cunningham Boycott, who became a celebrated land agent in Ireland and was later buried in the churchyard. The tower gives the impression of five brick cubes or boxes stacked on top of one another, in decreasing sizes. There are no embattlements. The individual buttresses supporting each cube are also stepped. The original sixteenth-century tower base consists of brick and flint, and this is where the brick vaults were later constructed by the Boycotts. Each cube of the structure has a pointed arched window and there is intersecting tracery in the west window above the mausoleum.

The nave and chancel are earlier than the tower, as indicated by the fourteenth-century pointed arched south doorway, the Y-traceried windows in the nave and the windows of the same date in the chancel. The arched braced roof of the nave dates from the fifteenth century, but the Victorians renewed the chancel roof. The fourteenth-century octagonal font shows carved ornamentation of alternating human and flower heads at its bowl base. The Boycott family donated the pulpit in the early nineteenth century and adorned it with brass memorial plates to themselves. The unusually large Decalogue boards are also Victorian but the screen is more modern, probably twentieth century. Both the sedilia and the piscina with cusped heads are fourteenth century.

Caston – The Church of the Holy Cross

Caston is situated off the A1075, about 10 miles north-east of Thetford. The church stands in a well-kept churchyard, near the village green and war memorial. It offers an interesting history of roof changes. From medieval times until 1852, it had a thatched roof; then the decision was taken to convert to tiles. However, owing to problems with a leaking roof, it reverted to a Norfolk reed thatch in 1973. A beautiful thatched roof now shelters the nave and a separate one the chancel, which is built at a lower level. Points decorate both ridges. After severe storm damage in the early twenty-first century, the thatch was re-dressed and protected with wire netting.

The church and buttressed west tower are fourteenth century and mainly constructed of flint. The tower is square and entry to the church

The Church of the Holy Cross, Caston, Norfolk

is gained through its west door, which has an ogee-headed arch. Directly over the doorway lies a three-light reticulated traceried window containing some medieval glass. The top section of the tower is plain, with small pinnacles perched at the corners. Inside, a spiral staircase leads to the ringing chamber and belfry, which houses six bells installed around the middle of the eighteenth century. The belfry windows have Y-tracery.

Entry to the church was formerly through a south door in the nave, but this has been blocked with an inserted window. The nave and chancel date from the fourteenth century but the majority of the windows are fifteenth century, as also is the two-storeyed north porch, now converted into a vestry. A priest's door leads into the chancel, between the two Y-traceried south windows. Buttresses support both the nave and the chancel walls.

The font stands on the north side by the vestry. It has a plain octagonal bowl and is thought to date from the fifteenth century. A chest with three locks in the nave is also possibly fifteenth century and could only be opened when the rector and two churchwardens were present, each holding a different key. In the past, it was a legal requirement to hold the books of the parish relating to the register of births, deaths and marriages. The fourteenth-century nave roof is scissor-braced but panelled with fifteenth-century boards decorated with gilded bosses and ribs. The chancel roof

Carved bench ends in the Church of the Holy Cross, Caston, Norfolk

was renewed in a Victorian restoration but constructed in a similar fashion to the one in the nave. The majority of the pews in the nave were installed in 1839 but there are a few medieval ones in the north-west corner with poppyhead ends and carved animals. The pulpit is Jacobean. The base of the former screen survives below the chancel arch. It once had a rood loft above, with a beam supporting the crucifix, with the Virgin and St John the Evangelist on each side. The turret housing that enclosed the stairs that led to it still remains visible on the outside north wall.

A striking feature of the chancel is the large brass chandelier holding eighteen candles that reputedly once hung in Hampton Court Palace, before Charles I gave it to Cheshunt Church in Hertfordshire. It came from there to Caston as a donation in 1871. Several of the stalls in the chancel are medieval, and two for the clergy have misericords. The east intersecting-traceried three-light window contains much Victorian glass but the centre light, showing the instruments of the passion, is perhaps medieval. In the south chancel windows are Victorian medallions of the symbols of the four evangelists: St Matthew's winged man, St Mark's lion, St Luke's ox and St John's eagle.

Claxton – St Andrew

Claxton is about 9 miles south-east of Norwich and is best reached off the A146 road to Lowestoft. St Andrew's church lies in an isolated position.

A reed thatched roof with a scalloped ridge covers the nave, but the chancel is tiled. The walls consist mainly of flints but several of the windows and quoins are bordered with brick.

There is a fourteenth-century square west tower but the unembattled upper section may be fifteenth century. There is one tiny pinnacle on each corner making four in total on the tower top. The bell openings, with rounded heads, are louvred and below are small lancets. The tower is unbuttressed. The brick south porch, which has a tiled roof, dates from the late fifteenth or early sixteenth century. It has a wide hood-moulded Tudor arch with an empty niche above, once filled no doubt with a statue of St Andrew. A white trellis gate now guards the porch entrance. The Norman nave once had a north aisle but it has been demolished and the three bays of the arcade blocked, but there is still a north door. Clear glass fills the leaded-light windows; most have two lights but the east window has three.

The whitewashed interior contains the royal arms of George I, who reigned during the early part of the eighteenth century. Four lions support the sturdy stem of the fifteenth-century octagonal font, which stands on a small pedestal. Four of the panels depict carved shields, including the saltire cross, (often called St Andrew's Cross), the instruments of the passion, an emblem of the trinity and two lions and flowers. There are some old box pews in the nave but many have been cut and reduced in size by the Victorians to form the plain benches that line the aisle. The chancel, with a small altar table was rebuilt in 1867 but still retains its original piscina of 1300 and a large memorial tablet to Sir Henry Gawdy, who died in 1620.

Coltishall – St John the Baptist

Coltishall is on the B1150 about 9 miles north of Norwich. The parish church of St John the Baptist stands in a large walled churchyard. A continuous Norfolk reed roof sweeps over both nave and chancel, with the ridge decorated with points. The roof is due to be rethatched during 2006 with the assistance of an English Heritage lottery grant. The large area of roof makes it an expensive proposition.

The church has a Perpendicular flint west tower that rises to a height of 67 feet. Tall buttresses support the corners of the square structure.

St John the Baptist, Coltishall, Norfolk

St John the Baptist's font, Coltishall, Norfolk

There is tracery in the louvred bell openings, and small separate lancet windows below shielded with lattice. The belfry houses six bells, one of which dates from 1624. The tower is embattled and also has a clock, fitted in 1877, with just two faces, one to the north and one to the east.

The Perpendicular north porch has a leaded roof, whilst the south one is tiled. The vestry, which was added in 1877, has a slate outshot roof. The walls of the nave and chancel consist mainly of knapped flints but the north wall contains a few red tiles and bricks that were salvaged from a Roman ruin.

The west door gives entry to the church. The square Purbeck marble font has four shallow arched panels lightly recessed on each face, with no ornamentation. Four marble shafts around a sturdy central column support the bowl; the square plinth below also consists of Purbeck marble. An unusually colourful red, green and gold painted lid covers the font.

There is a fourteenth-century arcade that replaced the original south wall, when the south aisle was added. The ceilings are of eighteenth-century plaster.

A Stuart period domestic table forms the simple altar of the lady chapel. The ancient tapestry screen behind it was obtained in 1918, after it was salvaged from a Belgian church destroyed during the First World War. There is a hood-moulded stoup in the south wall and several

Anglo-Saxon windows in St John the Baptist, Coltishall, Norfolk

memorials may be found on the south aisle floor. The pews are plain, with the needlepoint kneelers boasting a variety of colourful patterns. There is a seventeenth-century west gallery.

The Victorians inserted an unusually large circular window in the north wall of the nave. However, it now contains some ancient stained glass obtained from a continental church that was destroyed in the Second World War, in memory of Annabel and Arthur Morse, who died in 1955 and 1959 respectively. Immediately above the large circular window there are two tiny round Anglo-Saxon windows set in individual splayed recesses. The fifteenth-century chancel screen has undergone much restoration and has tracery above its arches. The modern stained-glass east window behind the altar shows Christ the King, Mary Magdalene, King Edmund and others. The sanctuary contains a three-seat sedilia with cusped arches above.

CRANWICH – ST MARY

Cranwich is situated about 10 miles north-west of Thetford and lies on the A134. St Mary's parish church stands on a mound surrounded by trees in an overgrown circular churchyard; the closeness of the trees encourages moss formation on its thatched roof. The church is normally left open.

St Mary, Cranwich, Norfolk

It has a Saxon round tower constructed of flints, with some brown carstone in the base. The tower was probably built in two stages during the Saxon period, the lower section being earlier than the slightly tapering top one. The battlements were a later addition because during the Saxon period a conical thatched roof may well have cloaked the tower top. Gargoyle faces stare out just below the battlements.

Individual Norfolk reed thatched roofs, with straight flush ridges now cover the nave, chancel and south porch, as they have for most of St Mary's long history. However, during the nineteenth century slates did replace the thatch and stayed until 1973, when they deteriorated and the roofs reverted to thatch. There are two sets of bell openings in the tower; the lower circular ones with central knot patterns are probably of the eleventh century. The upper ones with arched louvred openings are later. A small round window in the base of the tower looks westwards and may be the oldest.

The south door, which leads into the nave, dates from around 1200 and the hood-mould over its arch has dogtooth carvings. A rendered fourteenth- or possibly fifteenth-century porch, with a wide arched entrance, now protects it from the weather. There is also a blocked north doorway in the nave that may be late thirteenth century. The original tower arch is also blocked. Buttresses support the walls. The windows are mainly fourteenth or fifteenth century, with the exception of one older small lancet

St Mary's font and harmonium, Cranwich, Norfolk

window in the nave and the Victorian three-light east window. The chancel windows are mainly Y-traceried.

The floor of the church is chiefly composed of bricks. The plain octagonal font, supported on a substantial stem, dates from around 1300. A harmonium, possibly late Victorian, stands next to it with the assurance inscribed on its pedal that is 'mouseproof'. All the pews and stalls form part of a Victorian restoration and have poppyhead ends. The pulpit is also nineteenth century. There is a memorial on the north chancel wall to Revd John Partridge, who was the incumbent during the restoration. The piscina in the sanctuary south wall dates to about 1300.

Crostwight – All Saints

All Saints, the parish church of Crostwight, is located in the north-east of Norfolk, mingling with a cluster of other thatched churches, such as Paston, Bacton, Edingthorpe, Hempstead, Brumstead and Lessingham. Crostwight is best reached off the A149, at the junction with Dilham. A rough grass path at the side of the Old Rectory leads to the isolated

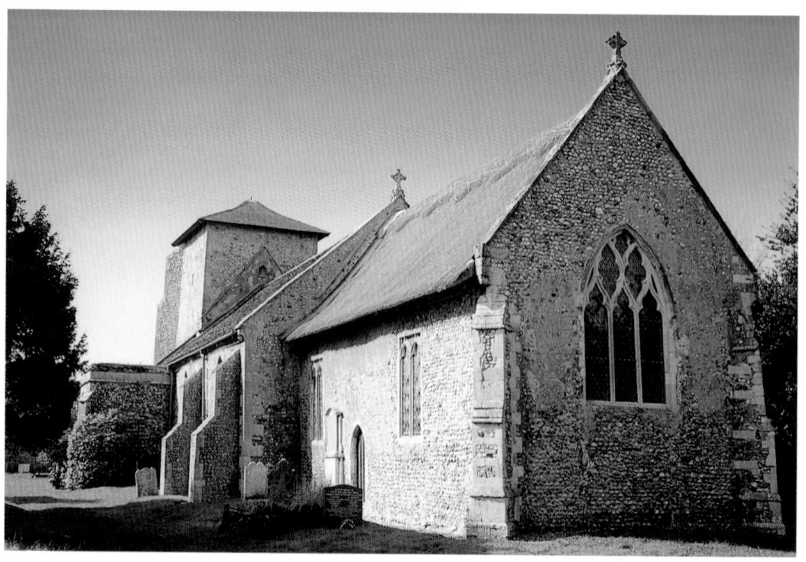

All Saints, Crostwight, Norfolk

church, a walk of about 40 yards. The church is normally locked but the key-holder lives at the Old Rectory. A wall surrounds the churchyard.

The chancel boasts a thatched roof with scallops on the ridge, but the nave is tiled. However, the outline remains of a high-pitched roof are still visible on the east exterior wall of the tower, suggesting that the nave might also once have been thatched. Both nave and chancel gable walls bear crosses on their tops. The walls of the church and the tower consist of flint cobbles and knapped flints. A leaded flat roof shelters the south porch, also built with flints.

The large buttressed west tower appears squat because the top section became unsafe and was removed in 1910. This explains the unusual look of the truncated tower, topped with a low red pyramidal roof. The tower has a west window and small bell openings; the bells had to be lowered when the top section was demolished. The tower and church both have their origins in the fourteenth century. The leaded-light windows, fitted with clear glass in both nave and chancel, have Y-tracery. The Victorians inserted the east window.

The entrance door into the church is narrow, just 4½ feet. The outstanding feature of the interior must be the large number of fourteenth-century wall paintings on the north wall. At the western end, there is a depiction of the seven deadly sins growing on a tree emerging from the mouth of Hell. It is interesting that medieval teaching favoured the number seven for a wide variety of religious themes, such as the seven sacraments, the seven gifts of the holy spirit, the seven sorrows of the Virgin, the seven virtues and the seven works of mercy; the creation also took place in seven days. To the right of the seven deadly sins there is a St Christopher. Further along the wall a long series of paintings depict the passion, starting with Christ's entry into Jerusalem and continuing with scenes prior to the crucifixion and then concluding with the ascension.

Near the paintings, an octagonal thirteenth-century font made of Purbeck marble stands with eight outer columns supporting it on a two-step pedestal. Open-backed pews with poppyhead ends line the single aisle. The chancel arch is probably fourteenth century but the carved wooden screen is a little later. Carvings of winged hearts may be seen, together with other motifs, on the dado, which is possibly of the fifteenth century. The hearts, of course, depict Christian love, understanding, joy and sorrow. The upper part of the screen is later. There is no electricity and the church is lit only with lamps and candles.

EATON – ST ANDREW

The thatched church of St Andrew is remarkable. It is the only thatched church in the city of Norwich; indeed it is extremely rare to discover a thatched one in any city or large town in England. It consists of two parts: a medieval section dating from the thirteenth century and a new centre that was consecrated by the Bishop of Norwich in 1993. The church is situated in Church Lane, Eaton, in the southern suburbs of Norwich and may be reached off the A140. It has a lychgate that was installed in 1887. Before the 1980s, it stood in open country, but spreading suburbia finally engulfed it.

A Norfolk reed roof, with a straight ridge of sedge, covers the nave and chancel, and a separate similar thatch shelters the north porch. Both are due to be rethatched in 2006 at a cost approaching £90,000; over 3,000 bundles of Norfolk reed will be required. Depending upon conditions, this new Norfolk roof should last from fifty to seventy years, although the sedge ridge will need attention at shorter intervals.

The thirteenth-century church is mainly constructed of flints, bound together with lime mortar obtained from a local kiln. It has a square fifteenth-century Perpendicular west tower with diagonal buttresses. The top battlements have flushwork panelling, with small pinnacles perched at the corners. The bell openings are arched, with dual louvred openings. The tower window is traceried. The windows of the nave and chancel consist mainly of small thirteenth-century splayed lancets but the east window of the same date is of three lights, with intersecting tracery. The stained glass within it depicts Jesus calling St Andrew and other fishermen to be his disciples.

The north porch, which gives entry to the church, was added in the nineteenth century and just inside the church there are two stoups, one on each side of the door. During the nineteenth century, various fragments of fourteenth-century wall paintings were uncovered, including one of the martyrdom of St Thomas Becket in 1170. Others depict St John the Evangelist, St John the Baptist and a censing angel. Another over the south door appears to show two women, one of whom is holding a rosary. The scene probably represents Titivullus and the two gossips. Titivullus was a minor devil who kept a wary eye on worshippers who gossiped rather than paying attention to the mass. He often appears in medieval literature, as well as in idle gossip paintings that always depict women. As only one woman has a rosary, there may be an implication that the devil stole the other woman's whilst she gossiped.

Two painted consecration crosses still survive, one on the north wall of the nave and one directly opposite on the south wall. The fifteenth-century font was originally in Sandringham church but came to Eaton in 1896. Verses of Psalm 148 are inscribed on the trusses of the nave roof, which replaced the original. Below, Victorian pitch-pine pews once stood but these were replaced in the mid-twentieth century by donated oak pews. There are embroidered kneelers showing biblical and local scenes. Two blocked doorways conceal the stairs that once led to the rood loft. The timber screen dates from 1957 and has three arched openings. Oak tablets list the Ten Commandments on the chancel wall. The altar dates from the seventeenth century and is made of deal, with an oak top. The sanctuary contains a fourteenth-century piscina.

The small medieval church only accommodates eighty people, so it was enlarged in 1993 to increase the capacity to 300. The architect was Nigel Sunter. A large square worship centre, with some flint and stone, was built on the south side in a lofty, modern, spacious style, with a three-bay timber arcade and a gallery. Entry is through the old church. Laminated pine beams support the structure, which has three glazed gables facing east, south and west (see fig. 6). The floor of the new church displays a number of tiles that bear crosses; each one marks the spot where graves existed before the new church was built on top. On the bases of the four vertical support beams are carvings depicting Old Testament scenes: namely

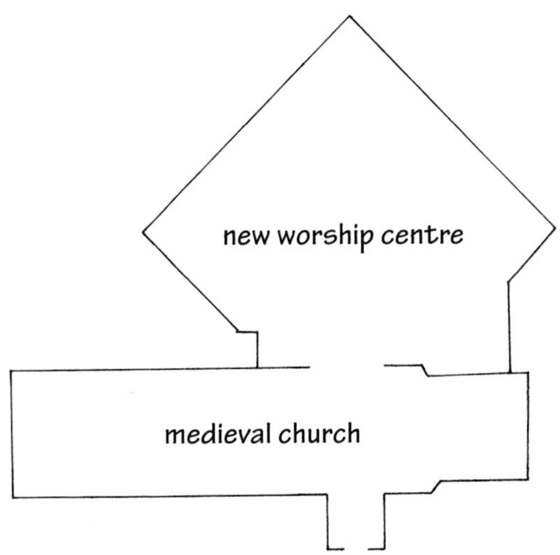

Fig. 6 St Andrew's Church, Eaton, Norfolk

the creation, Jonah and the whale, the parting of the Red Sea, and Noah's ark. A Norfolk craftsman, David Gregson, made the altar and other fittings in the new church. The new and the old churches are both used for services, which alternate between them. The good acoustics of the new church allow musical events also to be held there.

Edingthorpe – All Saints

This isolated thatched church stands outside the village on a low hill, surrounded by farmland. Some parts date from the twelfth century and others from the fourteenth. Edingthorpe lies about 3 miles north-east of North Walsham, off the A149, Cromer to Great Yarmouth road.

The whole of the church, including the tower and south porch, is constructed of flint. The porch entrance has a pointed arch, with an empty statue niche above, and the south doorway into the church is twelfth-century. A tiled roof covers the porch.

A Norfolk reed thatched roof covers the nave, with scallops and points on its ridge. A tiled roof shelters the small chancel. The late Saxons or early Normans built the round, tapering tower but its octagonal belfry top, containing two bells, dates from the late fourteenth century. The windows

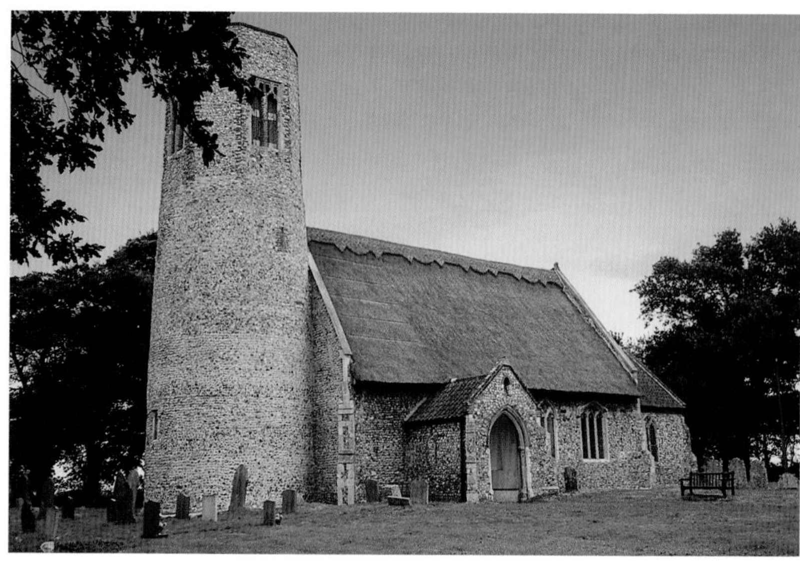

All Saints, Edingthorpe, Norfolk

Wall paintings at All Saints, Edingthorpe, Norfolk

of the church are all different, with tracery of varying types. All are of the Decorated or Perpendicular periods.

On the interior west wall is an old door that used to hang in the twelfth-century north doorway. It had to be replaced because wet rot spreading from the base and woodworm slowly combined to destroy it. Expert opinion varies on its age; some suggest it is probably fourteenth century but others think it is possibly seventeenth century. The new plank door hung in its place in 2000 was an exact copy made by Joe Dawes of nearby Corpusty. The church has a tiled floor with plain pews lining each side of the single aisle. The fourteenth-century octagonal font has quatrefoils on the bowl, with a panelled and traceried stem. It stands on an octagonal pedestal, with two steps. There is also a rustic reader's desk that is dated 1587 and a pulpit dated 1632. A painted piscina niche may be found near the pulpit. There is also a wrought-iron hourglass stand that was used to remind the priest not to give an overlong sermon.

There are some fourteenth-century wall paintings on the north wall. In one, St Christopher carries the Christ child over the water. Another in a fragmented, faded condition depicts the six works of mercy as the branches of a tree. There is also a fourteenth-century painted frame around a tall statue niche directly over the entrance to the rood loft stairs, by the chancel arch. A series of small rosettes decorates the margins around

The rood screen in All Saints, Edingthorpe, Norfolk

the frame and the interior of the niche is also painted. The magnificent and rare rood screen also dates from the fourteenth century. The top section consists of shafts with pointed arches. The six panels at the base are adorned with paintings of six saints, with their attributes. Viewing left to right they are St Bartholomew with the knife with which he was flayed, St Andrew with a cross in the shape of an X, St Peter with the keys of the kingdom of Heaven, St Paul with the sword by which he was executed, either St John or more probably St Catherine of Siena with book and palm leaf, and St James the Greater, with staff and scallop pilgrim's shell.

Outside, a low double bank which may have once formed part of an ancient earthwork defensive system, surrounds the churchyard. A former rector built the lychgate as a memorial to his son, who lost his life in action during the First World War. He went down with his ship when it was torpedoed in the Mediterranean, on 13 August 1915. The lychgate also stands in gratitude to the other parishioners who sacrificed their lives during the Great War.

Filby – All Saints

Filby lies about 7 miles north-west of Great Yarmouth on the A1064. All Saints church has a reed thatched nave roof decorated with scallops, with

All Saints, Filby, Norfolk

slates covering both chancel and porch. Leaded flat roofs shelter the two side aisles alongside the nave, just below the thatch eaves level. The spacious flint-walled church is a good example of a prosperous wool church; it has a Grade 2* listing. Wool churches arose when some of the vast wealth accruing from the trade in wool and cloth in late medieval times was lavished on them. All Saints dates mainly from the middle of the fourteenth century but has fifteenth-century alterations, including the tower. The north porch was added in the nineteenth century.

The square flint west tower has crow-step battlements and instead of pinnacles the corners are topped with figures representing the four Latin doctors, the fathers of the Church: St Ambrose, St Jerome, St Gregory and St Augustine. There are large two-light louvred bell openings in the buttressed tower, with tracery above. Below on each side of the tower, there are tiny quatrefoil windows with hood-moulds. Bands of iron cross and recross the tower door and seven locks fasten it.

Entry is through modern glass doors at the west end. Coloured tiles cover the floor of the interior. The church underwent extensive restoration between 1873 and 1879 and this is the period from which most of the stained-glass windows originate. Another restoration took place in 1886. The two-light leaded clear glass window in the north aisle has four stained-glass inserts showing the miracles and life of Christ, including carrying the cross to Calvary and the ascension. The interior of the church has two arcades of five bays, with octagonal piers supporting the pointed arches, which results in three aisles. Attractive pews line them. The lady chapel in the south aisle has a stained-glass window behind the altar.

The octagonal font on its similarly shaped pedestal dates to the Early English period, the mid-thirteenth century. It therefore predates the present church. It has eight supporting columns spaced around a central shaft, and a flat wooden cover. It is made of Purbeck marble, which is not a true marble; as I have said, it consists of fossilized limestone derived from freshwater snails. There are stoups beside both the north and the south doors. The polygonal pulpit dates to the sixteenth century and the lectern is made of brass. The church also contains an old red harrow, a reminder of the agricultural heritage of East Anglia.

It is thought that the dado of the chancel screen dates from the mid-fifteenth century. It depicts various saints, four on each side, from left to right: St Cecilia with her garland, St George fighting the dragon, St Catherine of Alexandria with her wheel, St Peter with the keys to the Kingdom of Heaven, St Paul with sword and book, St Margaret of Antioch with her cross and dragon, St Michael weighing souls, and St Barbara with the tower where her father imprisoned her. The top rail of

The chancel screen, All Saints, Filby, Norfolk

the dado shows carved vine ornamentation. The chancel contains several monuments and also an organ. The choir stalls have poppyhead ends.

In the past, it is understood, people with the name Filby travelled from afar to meet in the church to celebrate on special occasions.

FRITTON – ST EDMUND

Fritton lies some 5 miles south-west of Great Yarmouth on the A143, close to the Suffolk border. St Edmund's parish church has a flint round tower of Saxon origin, and it once stood alone, probably for defensive purposes. The Saxon apsidal chancel was also separate, probably used as a wayside chapel dedicated to St John the Baptist. Later the nave was added by the Normans to create an integrated church. The tower contains one bell, dated 1508. An unusual feature of the flint church is its lack of symmetry; the apsidal chancel is not in line with the centre of the Norman nave and the latter is not centred with the tower. This is no doubt due to the fact that the three sections of the existing church were not built at the same time. The interior reveals a beautiful and fascinating chancel and sanctuary with ancient arches.

A reed thatched roof covers the nave and a separate thatch the chancel;

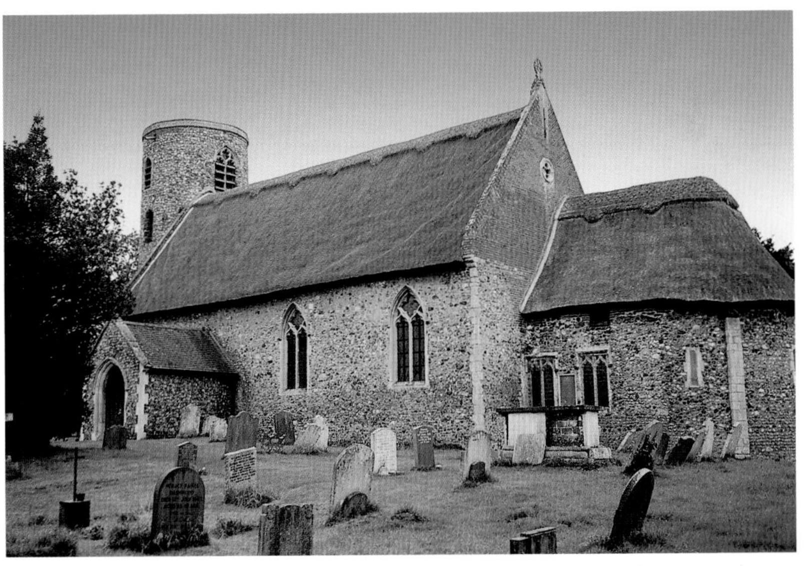

St Edmund, Fritton, Norfolk

both ridges are ornamented with scallops. The south porch has a slate roof sheltering its knapped flint walls and was erected in 1855, when restoration took place. Two straight flat buttresses support the rounded chancel wall, which has three slit windows, the centre one being the only Saxon original. The stone cross that sits on the top of the nave east gable wall dates from the twelfth century and is known as a *Rosa Crux*. It formerly adorned the chapel of the Bishop of Norwich's summer residence at Thorpe, before it was sold in 1929. The eastern end of the south nave wall carries an ancient mass sundial.

By the south door there is a niche that was formerly used as a holy water stoup. The font is a Victorian reproduction of a Norman design. The Jacobean pulpit is a rare plain panelled three-decker. The normal procedure was for the lessons to be read from the lower deck, the service to be conducted from the middle one and the sermon to be preached from the upper deck. There is a large fourteenth-century painting of St Christopher on the north wall of the nave, opposite the south door. He holds a staff in his right hand and carries the Christ child on his left shoulder as he wades west through the water, with a fish swimming near his foot. A red border encloses the whole picture. Another fourteenth-century wall painting of St John the Baptist enriches the east jamb of the south-east nave window. The traceried leaded-light

St Edmund's chancel, Fritton, Norfolk

windows in the nave are of two lights. The chancel screen also dates from the fourteenth century and has circle tracery over its ogee arches. However, the supporting shafts are Victorian replacements.

A step leads down into the enchanting chancel, which is low, dark and very atmospheric. It contains wall paintings over the sanctuary arch that date from the twelfth century and there is a red scroll pattern around the east window of the apse, also dating from the twelfth century. Victorian stained glass depicting various saints fill the slit windows of the apse, the middle one of St Edmund, the northern one of St Nicholas and the southern one of St Benedict. The other two-light windows in the apse also depict saints. Nearby stands a Norman pillar piscina and the altar table is Jacobean. The few choir stalls are ancient, dating from the thirteenth century, and some face east. The pews in the nave are Victorian. Above the south two-light windows of the chancel, there is a small chamber that was once reputedly used to store contraband; it was locally called the 'smugglers' loft'. The small entry to it may be seen on the outside wall above the windows.

Hales – St Margaret

Hales is about 12 miles south-east of Norwich and is reached from the A146. The remarkable little thatched church of St Margaret stands alone in the middle of open countryside, about ¾ mile south of the village. It is normally kept open and parking is relatively easy. It has been redundant since 1973 and the Churches Conservation Trust has cared for it since 1974. The church is remarkable because it has survived since the Normans built it in the twelfth century without undergoing any excessive change.

It consists of a round western tower, a nave and a chancel with a semicircular apse, supported by small buttresses. Apsidal chancels were very popular in the twelfth century but few still survive. The one at St Margaret's has decorative blind arcading between the buttresses.

A Norfolk reed roof covers the beautiful rounded chancel and also the nave. A parapet wall divides the two roof surfaces. The ridges of both are highly ornamented with scallops and points, some separate and others adjoining one another in a central pattern. A thatched apron extends below, ending just above the eaves. The lovely textured walls of the church are constructed with flint rubble, with a few Roman tiles and other materials incorporated into the mix. The Norman round tower has

St Margaret, Hales, Norfolk

Norman north doorway at St Margaret's, Hales, Norfolk

a flat roof; its small ornamented parapet and the louvred bell openings were added later.

Both south and north doorways of the church were fashioned with limestone imported from Normandy and are magnificent. The north one is more elaborately carved than the south. There are patterned bands of Romanesque motifs, such as foliage, zigzags or chevrons, stars and rosettes on the arches. The columns at the side, too, have decorative motifs on their capitals. The hood-mould over the door is ornamented with a chain of little wheels.

The major alteration to St Margaret's is in the windows. For example, the lancet windows and the single Y-tracery east window were inserted in the thirteenth century. The nave Y-tracery windows are also later additions, except for the one original blocked Norman window in the south wall of the nave.

The 43 foot nave has simple individual seats placed each side of an aisle, but contains a majestic late fifteenth-century font, with lions against the stem. The panels on the well-preserved bowl have carvings of angels holding shields and roses. The thin Jacobean font cover hides a strange silhouette figure on its base. Unfortunately, the cover has now been removed for security reasons and stored elsewhere. The nave also has an eighteenth-century west gallery built over the blocked tower arch. The interior of the church is light because of the clear glass in the windows; there is no electricity and there are oil lamp holders suspended from the ceiling.

The remains of several wall paintings survive. A huge fourteenth-century St Christopher welcomes visitors opposite the north doorway, by which the church is entered. It is rather faded but parts of the saint's head may still be seen, together with that of the Christ child. Both sides of the nave retain painted consecration crosses and a small recess that was carved into the reveal of the north-east window contains painted ornamentation of red and white squares, with foliage. Above the eighteenth-century pulpit, in the jamb of the south-east window, may be seen a figure thought most likely to be that of St James the Great, with a red foliage border painted above him on a white background. Incidentally, the rare three-decker pulpit was reduced in size towards the end of the nineteenth century.

There is a fourteenth-century painting of angels blowing the 'last trump' on Judgement Day on the spandrels of the high chancel arch; their trumpets point downwards to wake the dead. The chancel has some further painted images of consecration crosses, also scrollwork with red chevron patterns in a frieze over the east window; in addition there is decorative work in and around the niches by the stone altar, which still carries four consecration crosses and may be the original.

St Margaret's chancel, Hales, Norfolk

Only the lower part of the rood screen survives; the panels are painted alternately red and green, with only traces of colour remaining. Just one still has its traceried head. The stairs that led to the former rood loft still remain in the north wall but are now blocked. The chancel retains an aumbry, with its ancient wooden shelf, on the north wall, with a piscina on the south wall. Beside the latter, the low window-sill provided the seats for the clergy.

A similar type thatched church may be found at nearby Heckingham, and experts think that the same mason was also at work there to do the intricate crisp carvings around its south doorway.

Heckingham – St Gregory

Heckingham lies a couple of miles north of Hales and may be reached via the A146 and B1136, about 12 miles south-east of Norwich. The small Norman St Gregory's church stands in an isolated position on a mound above the River Chet. The church is redundant but the Churches Conservation Trust has cared for it since 1993. It is left open daily.

St Gregory, Heckingham, Norfolk

Individual thatched roofs cover the nave, apsidal chancel and porch. All the ridges have points and lovely thatched aprons extend below, finishing with inverted scallop shapes just above the eaves level. The thatch has obviously received attention since it was last renewed in 1978. Slates shelter the roof of the north aisle, which was built by cutting arches through the original north wall, possibly in the fourteenth century. The new exterior wall was constructed of brick with a little flint.

The Norman round tower is original only in its lower section; an octagonal section was built on top, possibly in the fifteenth or sixteenth century. The tower terminates in a plain unembattled parapet and the belfry contains two bells; the four bell openings are arranged symmetrically around the octagonal faces.

The outstanding feature of the church must be the magnificent south doorway, probably carved by the same mason who worked at Hales. It again displays Norman motifs such as zigzags and bobbins around the arches and the hood-mould above is ornamented with a continuous string of small wheels. The arches below have carved decorative capitals. The sixteenth-century porch that shelters it is built with brick and flint rubble and there are the remains of a blocked statue niche above the entrance.

The walls comprise a mixture of flint, rubble and brick, with stone dressings. Buttresses support the rounded apse. The only original

Norman windows to survive are in the apse, one each side of the early twentieth-century east window of the annunciation. On entering the church, which has a rather plain appearance, one finds a medieval stone coffin. The square font dates to the Norman period and has no ornamentation; a sturdy octagonal stem supports the bowl, together with four columns placed at each corner.

The interior was restored in 1899 but some of the old benches were retained, possibly dating to the sixteenth century. The floor of the north aisle has several stone coffin and ledger slabs. The sanctuary chairs are Jacobean.

Hempstead-by-Holt – All Saints

Hempstead-by-Holt lies 2 miles south-east of Holt and may be reached off the A148. A hedge and trees surround the church, which has a pretty small thatched apsidal chancel, which was added in 1926 through the magnanimity of Sir Alfred Jodrell. The reed thatched roof has a wide wire-netted ridge, ornamented with many cross-rods. The large east window, with an attractive hood-mould, came from the old chancel, which was demolished and contains Victorian stained glass.

Unusually, the tower lies to the north-west of the church owing to the demolition of the nave and the conversion of the south aisle into a new one. The tower was largely rebuilt with brick in 1744. The nave and chancel walls consist mainly of flint rubble, with some brick. The east end is buttressed and a cross sits on top of its east brick gable wall. All the windows were renewed in the eighteenth century, and the lancets in the chancel are edged with brick. Those in the nave are mainly of three lights. Tiles cover both the nave and the south porch. The south doorway into the church dates to the fourteenth century and has a hood-mould, indicating that the porch sheltering it was added at a later date.

Inside, there is a west gallery and a two-light window with tracery in the west wall. One old bench still survives, with a damaged poppyhead end. An angel standing on a globe ornaments an unusual late Victorian lectern, whilst the communion rail dates to the eighteenth century.

Hempstead-next-the-Sea – St Andrew

This church is built in a field. A minor road leads north-east to it off the A149 at Stalham, on the Cromer to Great Yarmouth road.

St Andrew, Hempstead-next-the-Sea, Norfolk

It is mainly built with flint cobbles and there is rendering visible on the outside of the buttressed nave wall. A cobbled flint wall surrounds the churchyard. The nave dates from the fourteenth century; the chancel may be a little earlier. The embattled square west tower was constructed with flint cobbles, with louvred bell openings. The impressive cobbled flint south porch has battlements and is unusually tall, reaching the top wall level of the nave. Buttresses support the corners and three lancet windows peep over the pointed arched doorway. There is also a priest's door.

A reed thatched roof covers the nave and a separate one shelters the chancel, which is at a lower level. The chancel is narrower than the nave. A straight ridge tops each roof. The nave windows, most with clear glass, are traceried, and the majority date to the fifteenth century. The east window consists of three lancets sharing the same surround and arch.

The interior of the church appears plain, except for its fine screen of unusual and intricate net tracery supported on slender shafts. The base depicts various saints, eight each side of the aisle. One painting shows a lesser known saint of the fourteenth century, St John of Bridlington with a fish in his hand. There is also a stained-glass window dedicated to him in Morely, Derbyshire. Another painting depicts St Erasmus, also known as St Elmo, being martyred by having his intestines removed by a windlass. Although little is known of his life, he reputedly became the

St Andrew's chancel screen, Hempstead-next-the-Sea, Norfolk

patron saint of sailors, with the windlass for his emblem. Later the windlass became confused with a machine of torture. St Elmo's fire, the luminous electrical discharge sometimes seen at ships' mastheads, is named after him. Another depicts St Juliana with a devil on a leash. She is reputed to have had a long conflict with the Devil, who tried unsuccessfully to persuade her to marry. All the paintings on the screen may be fifteenth century and were restored in the 1970s.

The fourteenth-century font, raised on a pedestal, has lions, shields and flowers ornamenting it. The pulpit is Jacobean and there is also a reader's desk. Benches line the aisle and a few have ornamented ends.

Horsey – All Saints

The closeness of the North Sea, just a mile away, ensures that Horsey Mere is the most brackish of all the Norfolk Broads and attracts some unusual birds and wildlife. The small village of Horsey is located near the marshes, about 10 miles north of Great Yarmouth, and is best reached off the A149 and the B1159.

All Saints, Horsey, Norfolk

The church consists of a nave and chancel in a single cell, a tower and a south porch. A continuous reed thatch runs over the nave and chancel, and the south porch is separately thatched. Scallops ornament the ridge, which was renewed in 1986; at the same time the porch roof was completely renewed. The thatch, protected with wire-netting will shortly need attention again; a thick layer of moss covers the north slope. The underside may be seen from the interior, adding rustic charm to the little church. Some parts date back to the Saxon period, such as the round tower and parts of the nave adjoining it. The walls of the church are built with rubble, cobbles and knapped flints.

The flint round tower rises to a height of about 40 feet, and was topped in the fifteenth century with a slender octagonal embattled belfry, bringing the total height to over 50 feet. The bell in the tower was cast in Norwich in 1597. The narrow louvred belfry windows are topped with trefoils. Owls are known to inhabit the belfry.

The south porch dates from the fifteenth century and boasts a moulded arch with the remains of a statue niche above. The south doorway into the church also has a moulded arch. In addition there is a fifteenth-century priest's door. The Victorians replaced many of the windows, one of the two exceptions being the thirteenth-century trefoiled headed lancet to the east of the priest's doorway, in the south wall of the chancel. The other is the two-light east window of the fifteenth century.

The Victorians carried out an extensive restoration of the furnishings, especially the stained-glass windows. The most unusual one must be that depicting local artist Catherine Ursula Rising, who died in 1890. She is shown dressed in red, standing at an easel with palette in hand, at the drawing-room window of Horsey Hall, which is situated about 100 yards from the church. Another Victorian memorial window, in the chancel, shows the Good Shepherd. One in the nave depicts St Paul, with his attribute, the sword, and another St Peter with the keys of the kingdom of Heaven.

The octagonal font may be fourteenth or fifteenth century and is ornamented with trefoil arches on the stem and bowl. The top of the bowl retains part of the iron staple to which the lid was originally fastened. The font stands on a single-step pedestal. The benches are Victorian replacements but a few constitute a mixture of nineteenth-century seats fitted with genuine fifteenth-century poppyhead ends. The choir stalls are completely Victorian but copy the medieval style. The carved wooden pulpit was installed in 1856, whilst the churchwarden's staves in the nave were made and placed in the church during the 1980s. The chancel screen dates back to the beginning of the sixteenth century but was restored in 1855. The arches are topped with fine tracery. The stairs leading to the former rood loft still remain in the north wall.

The Ten Commandments, the Lord's Prayer and the Apostles' Creed are prominently displayed in the sanctuary. They were painted on their metal backings in the nineteenth century. The south wall of the sanctuary carries a fifteenth-century piscina but its arch has lost its tracery. The nearby sedilia was possibly formed by lowering the window-sill to a convenient seat level. Three aumbries survive in the opposite wall but without their doors.

Hoveton – St Peter

Hoveton lies on the outskirts of the popular boating centre of Wroxham, on the River Bure. The thatched church is on the right-hand side of a narrow unmarked lane that branches left off the A1151, about a mile up the road when travelling north from Wroxham. It is normally locked but there is room for parking outside to view the exterior.

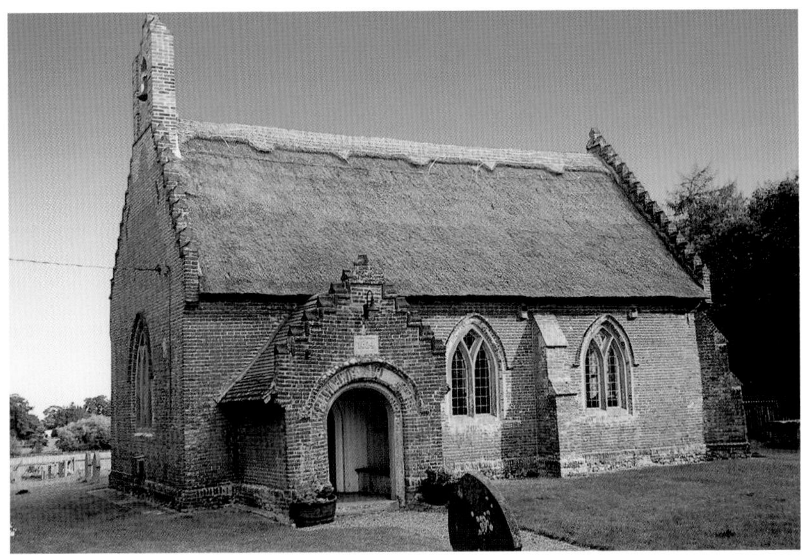

St Peter, Hoveton, Norfolk

St Peter's is slightly unusual. It was built in three bays entirely with handmade bricks instead of the usual flints that were so widely used for church building during many centuries in East Anglia. Brick buttresses also support the walls. Interestingly, little church building was carried out in the country when St Peter's was constructed in 1624, so it is also unusual in that respect. A reed thatched roof shelters both the nave and the chancel; scallops and points decorate the ridge. Both east and west walls are gabled and furnished with crow-steps. The open bell-cote above the west gable is also built of brick.

The brick porch has a crow-step gable and semicircular arches over the doorways but its roof is tiled. It is open, with no outside gate, only an inner door. The top bears the date 1624 on an inserted date stone. There is Y-tracery in the plain leaded light windows of the church, with brick hood-moulds above. The porch also has a brick hood-mould over the arch. The church has had at least two restorations, one in 1884 and the other after the Second World War, in 1947.

Exposed horizontal beams span the interior of the church, linking the north and south walls. The pulpit dates from the seventeenth century and was probably installed when the church was first built. It is polygonal and plain panelled, with the upper panels showing stylized palmettes. Benches line each side of the central aisle.

Ingworth – St Lawrence

Ingworth is situated 2 miles north of Aylsham and is best reached off the A140, Norwich to Cromer road. St Lawrence's church stands on a mound in the centre of the village.

It is mainly constructed of flint. A Norfolk reed roof with a straight ridge shelters the nave and a separate one the chancel, which was built at a lower level than the nave. The west round tower fell down in 1822 and parts of the stump were later rebuilt to convert it into a vestry. It was roofed with an attractive conical cap of thatch. The south porch into the nave also has a reed roof, so the entire church is thatched.

The porch consists of two storeys; the two-light upper window is headed with cusps and quatrefoils. Above the window, the gable wall is topped with stepped brick edging. The Norman nave was widened some time during its history, so it no longer lies in symmetry with the chancel and the vestry on the site of the old tower. A bell-cote sits on the top of the west gable wall, overlooking the vestry. A tall buttress supports the wall and is integrated into the south side of the vestry, thus binding the two together. The nave has large Perpendicular windows spanning the wall from near ground to eaves level on the south side. The small flint chancel has a priest's door in the south wall and narrow lancet windows in the north one.

The carved royal arms of William and Mary can be found on the west wall inside. The ancient octagonal font with a plain bowl stands on an octagonal pedestal. However, its cover dates to the twentieth century. The floor of the church is of bricks and a mixture of benches and box pews stands on it. The latter may date to the eighteenth century, as does the communion rail. The top section of the screen is eighteenth century; parts of the dado are much older. The east three-light window has intersecting tracery, with an inserted fifteenth-century Flemish stained-glass panel in the centre light depicting the presentation in the Temple.

Irstead – St Michael

This thatched church stands in an isolated position on a minor road, about 3 miles west of Potter Heigham, off the A149. Its location on a slight rise is similar to that of many other churches dedicated to St Michael.

The one at Irstead was built, mainly with flint, in the fourteenth century, with an embattled unbuttressed square west tower. However,

St Michael, Irstead, Norfolk

there are buttresses on both nave and chancel walls. A thatched roof shelters both the nave and the chancel. The thatcher, David Farman of A. E. Farman and Son, rethatched the roof in 1999, using Norfolk reed. The ridge was made with sedge, as is normal for a water reed thatch. Norfolk reed is difficult to bend over the apex of the roof because of its toughness. The ridge is straight and is ornamented with cross-rods, or cross-stitches as they are sometimes known. Before 1999, the roof was last fully rethatched in 1906, a glowing testimony to the longevity of Norfolk reed as a thatch material. However, ridges require replacing every fifteen to twenty years because they are not so durable as reed and are more exposed to the weather. The roof timbers of St Michael's do not have wooden battens, so a mat of interwoven reed was made to support the thatch. Locally, this technique is known as 'flaking' or 'webbing'. The underside of the woven matting makes an attractive feature, as it remains visible between the rafters from the interior of the church.

The south porch has a statuary niche in the gable. It contains an excellent but modern carved statue of St Michael fighting the devil, in the guise of a dragon or serpent. The inside arch of the south doorway still retains small pieces of original Norman zigzag ornamentation. The south door, decorated with medieval ironwork, is probably as old as the church.

Inside the church the traceried three-light east window shows the

St Michael's east window, Irstead, Norfolk

crucifixion in its central light, with a small stained-glass roundel above. The tracery at the arch top also has stained glass. The nave has a central aisle and a stone three-bay arcade to the south, with a lady chapel; there are leaded-light windows with attractive red glass surrounds. There is a monk's head on the sixteenth-century pulpit, and also linenfold panelling that is typical of the Tudor period. The panelling rises up the full height of the pulpit. The handrail was made from a medieval misericord.

The impressive font, on a two-step pedestal, dates from the fifteenth century, and statuettes decorate the stem. The octagonal panels around the bowl include various carved ornamentation, such as the head of Christ, the hand of God, the Lamb of God, the head of St John the Baptist displayed on a salver, and the sudarium or vernical of St Veronica, the cloth that she used to wipe the sweat from Christ's face, as he carried the cross to Calvary. The image of his face became miraculously imprinted on the cloth, which is now preserved as a holy relic in St Peter's, Rome. Traces of the original blue colour still survive on some of the surfaces of the font.

A large wall painting of St Christopher dominates the north wall of the nave, opposite the porch, and on the same wall there are also the remnants of an earlier St Christopher to the west of it. St Christopher was not only the well-known patron saint of travellers but he also protected against sudden death. It was popularly believed that whoever saw an image of St Christopher would not die that day. This is the reason why he is usually painted on the north wall opposite the porch, so that he would be seen by all who entered. The ancient dark benches lining the nave aisle have poppy-heads on their ends and the front ones bear various carved animals on the arms, including a hare and a dog or hound. Linenfold panelling may be seen on the back of one, suggesting a sixteenth-century date. The carved choir stalls have panelled backs and are seventeenth century. Directly in front of them, the base of the screen depicts the twelve apostles, six on each side of the aisle, painted directly on to wide wooden panels. A light speckled background highlights their tall figures. The sanctuary has a plain altar table.

Lessingham – All Saints

Lessingham is located about 3 miles north-east of Stalham and is best reached off the A149 Cromer to Great Yarmouth road. The thatched church is left open for visitors. It has a late thirteenth- or early fourteenth-century embattled square tower. It is constructed with flint cobbles, with no buttress support.

All Saints, Lessingham, Norfolk

A reed thatched roof covers the nave, the east part of which is now used as the sanctuary. The original chancel stands as a roofless ruin; it collapsed in 1961. Its walls still stand against the new brick gable east wall that was constructed to separate the two. The former aumbry may be seen in one of the ruin's walls. Except for the brick wall, the rest of the church, including the ruins of the old chancel, are built with flint cobbles. The porch has a pointed arch and a thatched roof, with a scallop decoration on its ridge. The main thatched roof of the church also has its ridge ornamented with scallops. All the roofs have recently been rethatched; it is estimated that the original thatch had lasted for about fifty years before it became no longer repairable, due to the disintegration of the ties holding the reeds down.

Church architect H. J. Green carried out a restoration of the nave in 1893 and the windows were replaced; nearly all of them were fitted with clear-glass traceried leaded-lights, with pinkish-mauve borders. However, there is one memorial stained-glass window in the present chancel that was originally part of the nave. The three-light window shows St Andrew the Apostle, St George and Richard the Lion Heart. The window honours the memory of:

> Locke Francis William Angerstein Kendall
> Lieut 9th Batt Norfolk Regt attached 21st
> Sqdn Cavalry Machine Gun Corps
> Died near Jerusalem 22 Nov 1917 aged 27.

Terracotta tiles cover the floor of this small plain church, which has no electricity. An ironwork lamp hangs from a beam of the ceiling. The inner roof is of the wooden plank wagon type. The octagonal pulpit probably stands in its original position but is in the area now used as the sanctuary. It dates from the sixteenth century and has a back panel and sounding-board. The Purbeck marble font, decorated with trefoils, has an iron ornamented wooden cover on top. Purbeck marble became a favourite material for English church decoration in the thirteenth century. Plain pews with straight ends line the single aisle.

The remains of the rood loft survive on the north wall of the present chancel. In the late 1960s, the Pilgrim Trust removed the base of the medieval wooden rood screen to restore it. It never returned to the church; it went on permanent loan to the Norwich Museums and was first exhibited at St Peter Hungate Church Museum, Princes Street, Norwich. It has now been placed in storage. It was made and painted around 1400,

Interior of All Saints, Lessingham, Norfolk

with some further panel paintings added in about 1555. Some of these were superimposed on top of some of the earlier painted figures. The panels depict various saints. The altar table commemorates the burial of Anne, wife of Edward Cooke, on 17 June 1634.

Mautby – St Peter and St Paul

Mautby lies about 5 miles north-west of Great Yarmouth and a minor road off the A1064 leads to it. The parish church of St Peter and St Paul has a reed thatched roof that stretches continuously over the nave and the chancel. Scallops and points decorate the ridge. Slates cover the porch, which was added in the nineteenth century. The Saxons or early Normans built its round tower of flints and made it unusually tall in comparison to other such towers in East Anglia. The octagonal belfry on top was built later. It has battlements and houses a single inscribed bell, dating from about 1500 and provided by the estate of Sir John Bataly of Acle. The belfry has louvred bell openings. The bottom, round section of the tower has a traceried west window.

The main body of the church is thirteenth and early fourteenth century and was built mainly with knapped flints; rendering now protects the

St Peter and St Paul, Mautby, Norfolk

outside chancel walls. The original priest's doorway still survives. The church once had a south aisle but it no longer exists. Margaret Paston, the wife of John Paston, was buried there. She was the daughter of John de Mauteby and lived at the hall during her childhood. After her husband's death, she returned in 1466 to Mautby and wrote many of the famous Paston letters, most of which are now preserved in the British Library.

The church claims that fragments of coloured glass in the north side windows of the nave are the oldest in Norfolk and date from the early thirteenth century. The stained-glass window with Y-tracery in the south wall of the sanctuary is dedicated to a former rector of Mautby, the Revd J. Norris Dredge. He served from 1896 to 1933. It shows two eucharistic scenes: one is of St Clare, the thirteenth-century foundress of the Order of Poor Clares, holding a monstrance. The other depicts St Thomas Aquinas, one of the first scholars of the Church and a Dominican friar in the thirteenth century, elevating the host. The monstrance, the vessel in which the host is exposed for veneration, is normally associated with the

Roman Catholic Church rather than the Church of England. For this reason, the window is probably unique.

The north chancel window depicts Our Lady and St Francis and commemorates the Dredge family. A Second World War bomb destroyed the stained-glass east window and it was replaced with one obtained from a Norwich church. It shows inset figures of St Peter and St Paul, to whom the church is dedicated.

The octagonal font of the fourteenth century has ornamentation on the tall sides of the bowl, and rib crockets decorate the later wooden cover. The church has a single aisle and tiles cover the floor. There are several memorials in the nave, and an ancient tomb of a Knight Templar in chain armour, with crossed legs, lies along the south wall. It is probably that of Sir Walter de Mauteby, who died around 1248. Unfortunately it is much defaced, probably during the Dissolution. The chancel arch is in the Perpendicular style. The base of the chancel screen dates from the fifteenth or sixteenth century but the Victorians added the upper parts. The choir stalls also date from the fifteenth century and have poppyheads. Some of the panels retain the carpenters' primitive mark numbering. The pews in the nave are plain ended. The sanctuary contains a sedilia and piscina.

Sedilia and piscina in St Peter and St Paul, Mautby, Norfolk

Old Buckenham – All Saints

Old Buckenham village boasts a thatched church, a large green, a castle, a windmill and a strong association with Australian cricket. It lies about 3 miles south of Attleborough on the B1077. Lionel Robinson, an Australian businessman and cricket enthusiast owned Old Buckenham Hall, until his death in 1922. There is a memorial to him in the chancel of the thatched All Saints church and his tomb is in the churchyard. Robinson was successful in inviting the Australian touring team of 1921 to play an English XI in the grounds of his home, on a wicket prepared with imported Australian turf. The match ended in a draw, when rain stopped play. Jack Hobbs, the first English cricketer to be knighted, rated the wicket as one of the best he had played on, despite the fact that he had to retire hurt after scoring 85 not out.

The thatched roof of the eleventh-century church covers both the nave and the chancel in a continuous stretch, with scallops decorating the ridge. The last rethatch took place in 1982; a scissor-beam roof supports the thatch. The north aisle was added in the fifteenth century, together with the south porch and both were given leaded roofs. A small medieval stone cross sits on the porch roof. The flint west tower, when it was first built in the eleventh

All Saints, Old Buckenham, Norfolk

century, was round but later the Normans converted it into its present octagonal form, using imported limestone to construct the shafts at the angles. The tower tapers from bottom to top; brick battlements were added in the seventeenth century. The bell openings alternate around the octagon faces with mock Y-tracery openings, which are blocked with knapped flints to increase the stability of the tower structure. The belfry houses six bells and a spire once topped the tower before a gale destroyed it in 1898.

The exterior west wall of the nave contains carstone blocks or puddingstones, which were often used for building by the Saxons and early Normans. The east wall is of Victorian brick supported by large buttresses, and the other walls are mainly flint, with some rendering on the south wall. There is a medieval priest's door in the south wall of the chancel. The north doorway is Norman, although it is set in the fifteenth-century wall of the aisle. It was probably transferred from another part of the church when the aisle was built.

Entrance to the church is via the south door, which dates from the fourteenth century, as also does its arch. However, on the interior nave side of the arch is a wider sixteenth-century arch, with a notice above stating: 'PROPERTY belonging to THE PARISH CHURCH of OLD

South doorway of All Saints, Old Buckenham, Norfolk

BUCKENHAM'. The nearby octagonal font dates from the late fourteenth century and has blank shields on it and beneath the bowl are carved eight grotesque, leering faces.

The north arcade has four bays, with the arches supported on ornamented piers; the north aisle is now used as a lady chapel. All the benches in the nave were installed in 1858; some were termed free and unappropriated, so that anyone could use them. They were furnished with plain bench ends, while the richer members of the congregation, who paid a reservation fee, sat on benches with fine poppyhead carvings. Some were fitted with half-doors, converting them into semi-box pews. The nave also boasts a bier reputed to be one of the oldest in the country, dating to 1655; it is of the drop-handle type. The large wooden pulpit has crisp carvings of flowers and cereals, which were completed in 1900 by Major William George Keppel, a staunch supporter of the church.

A large Victorian high arch leads into the chancel and above there are four stone carved faces; the two facing the nave are of Queen Victoria and Prince Albert, the two looking into the chancel are of an old man and a child of unclear representation. There was once a rood screen below the arch, and the blocked entrance to the stairs that led to the loft is still visible

Carved bench ends in All Saints, Old Buckenham, Norfolk

in the north chancel wall. Parts of the original screen base now form a partition to shield an area used as a vestry at the west end of the north aisle. All the choir stalls have poppyheads and on some there are small medieval figures of seated Old Testament prophets, including Jeremiah. There are also carvings such as St Matthew's winged man, St Mark's winged lion and St Luke's ox.

All Saints contains a variety of Victorian stained-glass leaded windows, in addition to the clear glass inserted in the north wall windows. There is an interesting stained-glass one of the good Samaritan, with a pelican below feeding her young. This alludes to the pelican piercing its breast to feed its young with its blood as a symbol of Christ's sacrifice on the cross. The traceries of the windows are fitted with fifteenth-century heraldic glass shields of the Knyvett family, who owned Buckenham Castle during that period.

Ormesby St Michael – St Michael

St Michael's church is easy to find as it stands right on the main A149 road, about 7 miles north of Great Yarmouth. A car park may be found next to it but the church is normally locked.

St Michael, Ormesby St Michael, Norfolk

Individual thatched roofs shelter the nave and south porch; scallops and points ornament both ridges. A raised flint parapet wall separates the thatch from the chancel roof, which is leaded. The thatched porch, constructed mainly of timber supported on a stone base, was added in 1973, when some further restoration got underway. Its apex lies just below the thatch eaves of the nave. The ridge and thatch of the porch is therefore subjected to extra rainwater cascading on to it from the main roof slope above. When possible, it is always better if the thatch of the main roof can be swept down continuously to form a canopy over a porch. Buttresses support the nave flint walls to the right of the porch.

The unbuttressed west tower, also built with flints, probably has Norman origins. It is square with a castellated top added in the fifteenth century and ornamented with knapped flint patterning. Lattices screen the pointed arched bell openings, which have later brick in-fillings at their bases, thus reducing their original size. The nave of the church is mainly fourteenth century, with an arched brace roof of the fifteenth century. The chancel roof may be a little earlier.

The Victorians carried out extensive restoration in 1885–6, including the renewal of the chancel arch and all the church windows. The ones on the south side of the nave have Y-tracery, whilst those on the north side have cusps. One two-light window in the south chancel wall has a quatrefoil in the top circle of its tracery. The east window has cusped tracery. The stained glass in the chancel windows is twentieth century and depicts the Christian message of faith, hope and charity, the three 'theological virtues', which are represented in the form of women. Charity is the most important of the three because the Church taught that charity was the love of God and the love of one's neighbour, and that the latter was of no real worth without the first.

The font dates from the thirteenth century and eight Purbeck marble shafts around a central column support the octagonal bowl. The use of eight gives an allegorical religious message, as we have seen, based on the belief that God created the Earth in six days and rested the seventh but the eighth day will be the day of judgement. The church retains several monuments. Several of the Pilgrim Fathers came from Ormesby St Michael.

Paston – St Margaret

Paston lies about 1 mile to the east of the B1145 and about 4 miles north-east of North Walsham. The small thatched church stands in the centre

St Margaret, Paston, Norfolk

of the village, which has strong associations with the Paston family. It is of interest that the village has never had an inn during its thousand-year history.

The Paston family became very powerful in the region during the fifteenth century and forged strong links, as benefactors, with Bromholm Priory at nearby Bacton, where there is also a thatched church. Their mansion once stood in Paston but has long since vanished. There are many monuments to them in St Margaret's church. The fame of the family relates to the Paston letters, most of which are preserved in the British Library. They were written between various members of the family between 1422 and 1509 and describe the history of that period, not only domestic and local affairs but also political events, such as the Wars of the Roses and the establishment of the Tudor dynasty. They form, therefore, one of the most important surviving sources of our knowledge of the life and manners of the period. More than a thousand letters were written, many by Margaret Paston to her husband John, a lawyer in London. In one, she relates how the Rector of Great Snoring in north Norfolk was arrested for murder and placed in stocks, awaiting his trial.

The local church, St Margaret's, dates from the fourteenth century and is mainly of flint pebbles with buttresses. A reed thatch shelters the nave, with a straight ridge and no ornamentation; this is a little unusual as most

Norfolk thatched churches have scallops and points. There is also a thatched lychgate on the west side of the churchyard in a rather distressed state, with vegetation infringing on it. It may once have been an entrance from the Paston mansion that stood beside the church, before the existing property was built on the site.

Slates cover the chancel roof. The windows have cusped Y-tracery, with some Victorian glass inserted. The flint porch, with a cross above, was added later in the fifteenth century, with mouldings around the semicircular arch of the door. The church also has a tall embattled square tower, flint built in three stages and buttressed. It has a ring of six bells. Various restorations have taken place: in 1601, 1843–4 and in 1869.

Just inside the south door are the remains of a stoup. Terracotta tiles cover the church floor. The fourteenth-century octagonal font has a panelled stem. The nave has a simple timbered roof, as it supports only the light load of the thatch above. There was once also a ceiling but the Victorians removed it during the 1869 restoration. The north nave wall carries a large fourteenth-century wall painting of St Christopher carrying the Christ child across a flooded river. Owing to its great age many parts have deteriorated, including the top of the saint's staff; however, fish

St Christopher wall painting in St Margaret, Paston, Norfolk

are still visible swimming in the water and also the orb in the Christ child's hand. Further along the same wall may be seen a depiction of the 'three living and three dead'. It shows a king, with two gentlemen or attendants, hawking in the woods and suddenly encountering three skeletons hanging and dancing in the wind. The message clearly highlights the mortality of man. Immediately below the painting there is a remnant of another, with a small figure probably depicting the 'weighing of souls' or the 'last judgement'.

A few old bench ends with poppyheads still remain in the nave, despite the Victorian restoration, which removed many of the old pews, replacing them with open benches. The Paston coat and crest ornaments one and the head of a horned devil another. The wooden chest at the rear of the nave has survived since the early fifteenth century. From more recent times, there is a memorial plaque on the north nave wall, donated by members of the Mediterranean Fleet in memory of Rear Admiral John Mack, who was killed on active service in 1943. The Mack family had always been great benefactors of the church.

There are also some magnificent stained-glass windows in memory of other members of the Mack family. The east window is dedicated to John Mack, who died in 1867, the south window to Lieutenant Commander Ralph Michael Mack, who went down with his ship, HMS *Tornado*, in action off the Dutch coast in 1917. The centre light of the window shows the figure of St Michael the archangel. There is also a Parish memorial north window in memory of the men of Paston who sacrificed their lives during the First World War.

The rood screen dates from the fifteenth century but has suffered much alteration. The rood loft doorway still survives. The chancel has a fourteenth-century piscina and sedilia, damaged when one of the large table tombs to the Paston family was installed. It was brought to Paston from Bromholm Priory, where John Paston was buried. There is also a huge memorial to Katherine Knevet, the wife of Edmund Paston, that was crafted by Nicholas Stone, the famous monumental sculptor of the early seventeenth century. The inscription states:

TO THE REVIVING MEMORY
OF THE VERTVOVS and
WORTHY LADY Dame KATHERINE
PASTON ... DEPARTED THIS
LIFE 10 DAY MARCH 1628
INTOMBED HERE EXPECTING
A JOYFVLL RESVRRECTION

Katherine Paston memorial in St Margaret, Paston, Norfolk

Behind the side of the altar, the texts of the Ten Commandments, the Creed and Lord's Prayer are displayed.

Finally, mention must be made of the magnificent thatched tithe barn that was built by Sir William Paston in 1581, and stands by the church. It measures 160 feet in length and is 60 feet high. A series of tie-and-hammer-beams support the massive thatched roof. The North Norfolk Historic Buildings Trust now owns it but English Nature manages it on their behalf. The barn is now home to barbastelle bats, one of the few colonies of this species in the United Kingdom.

Potter Heigham - St Nicholas

Potter Heigham is a popular yachting centre on the banks of the River Thurne, and its unusual three-arched bridge dates back to the thirteenth century. The thatched church of St Nicholas also dates to the thirteenth century. It lies just off the A149 Great Yarmouth to Cromer road.

A reed thatched roof covers the nave and a separate thatch shelters the chancel, which is smaller and lower. The east gable wall of the nave

St Nicholas, Potter Heigham, Norfolk

divides the two roofs. Both ridges are decorated at intervals with scallops, closely crafted on each side of the individual points. The single-storey south aisle abuts the two-storey nave wall, with the result that the line of six tall three-light top windows in the nave looks out over the aisle roof. A continuous hood-mould runs along the top of them. The flint round tower has an octagonal top, added in the fourteenth or fifteenth century. It is embattled and small pinnacles arise and ornament the centre of each of the castellations. The belfry has four bell openings with tracery.

The tall, impressive flint porch contains a statue of St Nicholas in a brick-framed niche above the entrance arch. There are two lancet windows in similar surrounds, one on each side. On entry into the church, the brick octagonal font immediately catches one's attention. It is a great rarity to find one of brick, rather than the normal stone or Purbeck marble. It dates from the fifteenth century and the bricks probably originated from one of the many local brickworks. A pulley lifts the font cover.

There are a number of fourteenth-century wall paintings in the church, including the works of mercy in the south aisle. The others are more difficult to interpret because of their poor condition, but one on the north wall is probably of St Christopher. A few of the benches date from the fifteenth century and have poppyhead ends; the others are Victorian. The chancel screen has painted panels depicting eight saints on its base or dado.

ROCKLAND ST PETER – ST PETER

Rockland St Peter is situated about 4 miles west of Attleborough and can be reached off the A11 and B1077. If the church is locked, there is a key-holder nearby; parking is available.

A Norfolk reed roof shelters the nave and extends over the small north and south transepts. The thatched roof caught fire in 1948, when rubbish was being burned in the churchyard. It so severely damaged the nave roof that it was replaced in 1950 with a new scissor-braced one. It was then given a new thatch with a straight ridge. The thatch has been repaired several times since but is now in need of a complete rethatch. It is estimated that the total cost would exceed £80,000. The fire also gutted the interior, including the pews, and the nave now only has chairs. Other furnishings have since been obtained from other churches, including the pulpit and chancel screen.

The flint round west tower survived the fire. There is some controversy over when it was built, ranging from the eleventh to the fourteenth century. The nave walls were constructed at the same time but the windows date from the fifteenth century. The tower consists of two round sections, the top one being of a smaller diameter than the lower. A round stair turret has been added to the north side and rises to the top. An octagonal unembattled

St Peter, Rockland St Peter, Norfolk

belfry perches on top of the tower, added in the fourteenth century. It has four ogee windows, which alternate around the octagon faces with blank arched filled-in openings. The belfry contains one bell, but the tower is unfortunately cracked and leaning so the bell cannot be rung. It would be interesting to know if this encouraged the bats that now inhabit the tower. Bats are now a protected species.

The north porch originates from the Norman period but underwent considerable rebuilding in 1624, which resulted in the use of red brick over the top of its gable wall. A cross sits on top. This porch is now used for entry into the church and there is a stoup just inside the door. The south porch was rebuilt in 1908 for use as a vestry and the small chancel also underwent a rebuild the following year. Both the porches and the chancel are tiled.

The octagonal font has tracery on its bowl and quatrefoils with circles around them on the stem. The beautiful tall fifteenth-century chancel screen came from a redundant church at Tottington and replaced the original, which was destroyed in the 1948 fire. There are finely carved ogee heads over its light divisions. The impressive rood beam above contains nineteenth-century figures of Christ on the cross, flanked by the Virgin and St John the Evangelist, which came from St Sampson's church in York. An arch shelters the entry to the chancel. The stained-glass east window was installed in 1909 and depicts among other images the good shepherd and St Peter's crossed keys.

Salhouse – All Saints

The picturesque village of Salhouse overlooks the lovely waters of the Broads, the water reed swamps of which for centuries have provided the materials for the thatching of cottages, ricks and churches. All Saints church stands on the north side of the village, when travelling from Wroxham on the B1140, in an isolated position behind the war memorial. Parking is available outside the church, which is normally kept locked. A tiled lychgate provides entry to the very large churchyard; the south porch of the church is also tiled.

A continuous thatched roof sweeps over the nave and the chancel, and the ridge is straight and unadorned. The roof supporting the thatch is of the crown-post type. Buttresses support the knapped flint walls of the church and also its truncated square tower. This fifteenth-century tower appears stocky because it was never completed, owing to lack of funds. It

All Saints, Salhouse, Norfolk

was built against the west wall of the earlier church's north arcade, but off the centre line of the present thatch ridge. At the time, it was hoped that the church nave could be enlarged. The remains of an arch may be seen on the east side of the tower, peeping over the north slope of the thatched roof. The height of the tower reaches just above the small quatrefoil sound holes. There are two bells, the oldest being from the fifteenth century. The battlements on the top of the tower were added later.

Inside the church, the north arcade dates back to the fourteenth century. It consists of five bays with octagonal piers supporting the arches. Most of the capitals have ornamental foliage, but one has the carved heads of figures. There is a small sanctus bell attached to the top of the rood screen, which would have been rung at the consecration of the host. This type of bell is now extremely rare. The Victorians replaced most of the stained-glass. The three-light window in the east gable wall has intersecting tracery; most other windows are fitted with plainer Y-tracery.

The sixteenth-century pulpit still has an hourglass stand that was used to remind the vicar not to speak longer than an hour, as it had been customary for sermons to last somewhat longer. The octagonal font, standing on its octagonal pedestal, originally came from nearby Woodbastwick's thatched church. It has a carved stem with a plain unornamented bowl. Some of the benches lining the aisle have poppyhead ends.

Scoulton – Holy Trinity

Scoulton lies on the B1108 about 6 miles north-west of Attleborough. The church is situated in The Street in the village. It is normally kept locked, but a key-holder may be found nearby. It has a wide variety of roofing materials; there is thatch on the nave, pantiles on the chancel, slates over the north and south aisles and lead on the porch roof. The thatch consists of Norfolk reed and has a pointed ridge. The two slated north and south aisles fit snugly under the eaves of the thatch. A small parapet wall separates the thatched nave from the tiled chancel.

The church was built of flint in the fourteenth century. It has a three-stage west tower with buttresses. The third stage, the belfry, is octagonal and sits on the two lower sections. The small brick parapet on the top of the octagon is unembattled. The bottom two stages are square with a Decorated leaded three-light west window. The Y-traceried windows in the nave and chancel are all fourteenth century, except for the Victorian restored stained-glass east window of five lights. The wide south porch, which gives entry to the church, was added in the fifteenth century and its buttresses contain flushwork ornamentation. A statue niche sits over the arched entrance, which has a hood-mould above. Fine wrought-ironwork decorates the impressive outer door, which is of the same date as the porch.

Holy Trinity, Scoulton, Norfolk

The interior of the church reveals two arcades on each side of the nave, consisting of three bays with octagonal piers supporting the arches. Both lead into chapels with individual altars. The font is octagonal and probably of the fourteenth century, whilst the pulpit, complete with sounding-board and back panel, is seventeenth century. The chancel has a recess with five deep holes in its stone slab base, possibly once used as cressets – receptacles for holding kitchen fat or grease, with a floating wick, used to provide light.

Seething – St Margaret and St Remigius

Seething is located about 6 miles south-east of Norwich, off the B1332. The church lies in a large well-kept churchyard, with a public gravelled footpath passing through it. A neat wooden fence surrounds the churchyard and the church is normally locked.

A reed thatched roof with a scalloped ridge shelters the buttressed nave, while slates cover the smaller chancel; slates also shield the south porch and the vestry to the north. A parapet wall separates the nave roof from that of the chancel. The church has a Norman round tower and is built mainly of flint rubble, with a little brick around the parapet. A slender lead spike with a weather-vane on top serves as a spire in the centre

St Margaret and St Remigius, Seething, Norfolk

of the tower roof. Bricks surround the large bell openings, which have rounded tops, and below there are lancet windows, also with rounded tops. In addition, the tower has a traceried west window.

The nave windows are of three lights, as is the east window, which contains Victorian glass showing St Paul, St Peter and St John. The other chancel windows have Y-tracery. The north chancel stained-glass window of an angel is fifteenth century. The others are of clear glass.

The porch leading into the church has an arched entrance and possesses a fifteenth-century arched brace roof. The font, also of the fifteenth century, has the seven sacraments on its bowl. The stem has four small statues ornamenting it.

The interior walls of the church are decorated with several fourteenth-century wall paintings, including on the north wall a St Christopher and a 'three living and three dead'. As we have seen, the latter refers to the story of a king, who with two gentlemen or attendants was hawking in the woods, when they suddenly encountered three skeletons hanging and dancing in the wind. The message is to highlight the mortality of man. A further series of paintings depicts the life of Christ, from the nativity to the ascension. Another painting, further along the wall, may well be of St John the Baptist. There are several other faded images on the east wall that are difficult to decipher. One appears to show two women gossiping together on a bench with at least two devils with horned heads around them. One of the women holds a rosary and the smaller minor devil at the bottom of the painting has another, implying that he has just stolen it from the inattentive woman. He no doubt represents Titivullus, who listens to idle gossip, gathering dropped syllables that will be taken into account at the day of judgement, when the gossip's soul is weighed. The larger devil at the top of the painting may depict Satan who encouraged the gossiping to deflect the women from prayer.

The base of the chancel screen dates from the fifteenth century, but a local man carved the top section in 1895. The door-frame of the stairs leading to the former rood loft still survives. The chancel contains a vestry off the north wall, a piscina and a window sill sedilia.

Sisland – St Mary

There are very few houses at Sisland; the parish is one of the smallest in Norfolk, with just over forty inhabitants. It sits north-west of Beccles and is best reached off the A146 road to Norwich. The church is normally left open for visitors between April and October, from 9 a.m. to 5 p.m.

St Mary, Sisland, Norfolk

It arose from the ashes of an earlier church, after lightning struck and destroyed the main structure in 1761. The ruins of the old church may be seen alongside the north wall of the present one; parts were incorporated into the new church, which was constructed shortly after the disaster. The salvaged flint rubble is mainly found in the north wall, together with a filled-in arch.

A well-cared for reed thatched roof with protective wire-netting shelters both the nave and the chancel. The ridge is ornamented with alternating scallops and points, joined together in a long continuous string. A delightful little thatched apron, also with scallops and points, decorates the base of the wooden square west bell-tower. The thatched roof extends both sides of the bell-tower, so that it appears to be perched on the thatch. This tower is small and weatherboarded, with pinnacles and a lead needle spire or spike in the centre of its roof. A weather-vane perches on the top of the little spire. The bell openings are round-headed and criss-cross pattern louvres shield them.

The small church is constructed of brick, with a little flint. Heavy buttresses support the walls, parts of which are rendered. Nearly all the walls and numerous buttresses are whitewashed, with the exception of the door surrounds and the arches over the windows, highlighting the exposed brick as a decorative feature. A cross sits on top of the east gable wall. The windows have Y-tracery and the west one has an etched farm scene to the memory of

Frederick John Haylock. The stained glass in the east leaded two-light window is much older and set in roundels, one of which depicts St Peter with his key, another St Paul with a sword by which he was beheaded and above them a dove symbolizing the Holy Spirit. A yellow stained-glass border surrounds each light. The only window in the north wall is in the chancel.

The church has a single aisle with plain benches each side; a west gallery supported on iron pillars overlooks them. The octagonal font, with a sturdy stem, dates from the fifteenth century and is decorated with carvings of lions, angels and flowers. The cover is seventeenth century, simple and slim. The chancel arch is supported by plain columns that divide it into two pointed arches. The list of rectors goes back to the thirteenth century, suggesting that the original church was Norman.

South Burlingham – St Edmund

South Burlingham is located about 10 miles east of Norwich and it is reached via the A47 and the B1140. The church is normally locked. It is fairly large, with a reed thatched roof sheltering the nave, chancel and south porch. The continuous thatched ridge sweeps over the nave and down a small step over the chancel, whose roof level is at a lower level than the nave.

St Edmund, South Burlingham, Norfolk

The square Perpendicular west tower is constructed of flints, as are the walls of the church. Diagonal buttresses support the tower corners and the east corners of the chancel gable wall are also buttressed. The tower has stepped embattlements and wide louvred bell openings, with pointed arch hood-moulds. These were most likely rebuilt during a nineteenth-century restoration.

The thatched porch is constructed mainly of flint, but there is some brick on the front elevation. The underside of the thatch may be seen from within the porch, lying on cross-webbed matting. The windows in the nave and chancel have Y-tracery, except for the east one, which has intersecting tracery. They are all from the late thirteenth or early fourteenth century and are fitted with clear leaded glass. The Norman doorway arch is decorated with zigzags. There is also a less elaborate Norman north door, which is now blocked.

The underside of the thatched roof may be seen from within the church; like the porch, it takes the form of decorative thatch matting. The octagonal font is thirteenth century. There are two wall paintings, a faded St Christopher on the north wall and a large depiction of the murder of St Thomas Becket in Canterbury Cathedral in 1170 on the south chancel wall. Both were painted in the fourteenth century. St Edmund's also has a lovely carved ornamented pulpit, with some paintwork, with a Jacobean backboard and tester. There is also decoration on the intricate chancel screen, with wide lights and ogee arches, tracery above and paintings on the lower dado half of the screen. Some of the benches have poppyhead ends, others have carvings of animals, birds and human heads, and there is also an elephant and castle.

Stockton – St Michael and All Angels

This is a small thatched thirteenth-century church, with a round tower, just to the west of the A146, about 3 miles north-west of Beccles. It is normally locked, but there is a key-holder nearby. A black metal rail fence encloses the tiny churchyard.

The continuous thatched roof covers both the nave and the chancel. Stephen Letch Thatchers of Tharston rethatched the roof in 2004 and topped it with a straight ridge. They used a water reed that was harvested in Walberswick, just over the border in Suffolk. It is understood that the previous Norfolk reed roof lasted for sixty years, a tribute to the quality and longevity of the reed.

St Michael and All Angels, Stockton, Norfolk

Rendering shields the Norman embattled round tower, which has an unusual slim lead spire recessed into the top. The Revd Valentine Lumley added it to the tower in the eighteenth century so that he could view the top of the church from his vicarage, which stood several miles away at Bungay. The tower has a sixteenth-century west window of two lights, and the louvred bell openings above have small round openings at their heads.

The buttressed walls of the church consist of brick with patches of rendering, as does also the south porch, which was added in the sixteenth century. It is a little unusual to find a brick-walled church, rather than the flint so widely used in Norfolk. In the seventeenth century, the porch was altered and the front was fitted with an attractively shaped gable. Tiles cover the porch roof.

The windows of the church are mainly leaded, with two or three lights, and vary in date from a late thirteenth-century lancet window to several of the sixteenth century. Some retain fragments of their original medieval stained-glass. The traceried three-light east window contains late Victorian glass.

The octagonal font dates from the fourteenth century and contains images of the evangelists. Its bulky stem stands on a heavy square pediment. The tall, attractive cover, rising to a rounded point, is decorated with crocketing. It dates to the early seventeenth century. The benches in the church have poppyhead ends and some date to the fifteenth century; the others are Victorian. The roof of the nave and chancel is arched brace.

STOKESBY – ST ANDREW

Stokesby lies about 6 miles west of Great Yarmouth and 2 miles east of Acle, and can be reached off the A47. St Andrew's church stands in a field about a five-minute walk from the village post office, along a path by farmland.

The church consists of a continuous reed thatched roof over the nave and the chancel, a south porch and a square, unbuttressed embattled tower. A series of small points ornaments the thatch ridge, and the underside of the thatch may be seen on the battens from inside the church, making an attractive feature. The west tower of flint and rubble dates from the Early English period and contains a single bell. The brick battlements on top were added in the early sixteenth century and were furnished with crow-steps. The louvred bell openings have Y-tracery.

The porch has a tiled roof and the walls were built with brick in the early nineteenth century. It was restored in 1985. The south door contains

St Andrew, Stokesby, Norfolk

Thatch underside at St Andrew, Stokesby, Norfolk

iron ornamentation at its centre by the knocker. The walls of the chancel and nave are constructed of flint and rubble and are buttressed. The windows originate from the Decorated period, with the exception of the Perpendicular one in the south wall. Most of the leaded-light widows are fitted with clear glass, but there are two of stained glass. A major restoration of the church took place in 1856 and 1858, with a further one of the chancel during the period 1910–5.

Six columns around a central shaft support the nineteenth-century plain square font. The carved oak pulpit comes from the same period and has a sounding-board. There is also a small organ. Most of the plain benches lining the paved aisle are Victorian but at the west end of the nave there are a few ancient ones with poppyheads. Grotesque carvings of animals such as hounds, eagles, lions and griffins ornament the arms. The griffin has the head and wings of an eagle on the body of a lion. In Dante's *The Divine Comedy* it represents Christ, in his dual nature as God and man. One bench, with a hound, has the initials RW carved on its end. Another arm depicts a woman in prayer. Varying types of tracery pierce the backs of these benches.

The Victorian choir stalls also have poppyheads and carved foliage. The wooden chancel screen of dado height is carved. The sedilia consists of three seats at different levels recessed into the window-sill. An

Carved bench ends in St Andrew, Stokesby, Norfolk

interesting brass on the chancel floor shows a knight in armour, with his wife at his side. There are also other brasses on the floor.

Taverham – St Edmund

Taverham is situated about 4 miles north-west of Norwich and lies just south of the A1067. St Edmund's parish church lies in a pleasant churchyard, bordered by trees. In the wood opposite the church, several skeletons have been discovered in the past, all hurriedly buried during the Black Death, which struck Norfolk so badly in 1349, killing about a third of the population – well over 50,000 people. Another misfortune arrived in 1459 when lightning struck St Edmund's church and severely damaged it. The nave was later rebuilt in the Perpendicular style.

A Norfolk reed roof formerly sheltered both the nave and the chancel, but tiles now cover the nave, although the chancel still remains thatched. The west tower was built in two stages, the lower round section in the eleventh century and the embattled octagonal top in the fifteenth. The latter has round headed bell-openings. The nave still retains its plain arched Norman north doorway. The south porch was rebuilt during 1861–3, as were the south aisle and arcade. Buttresses support the exterior walls.

The octagonal font bowl is decorated with shields, together with the symbols of the evangelists; eight small statues of saints support the stem. Most of the benches are plain, but there are two with poppyhead ends. There is a medieval screen with ogee arches and the fourteenth-century chancel has a blocked north doorway that once led into a vestry. The choir stalls have poppyhead ends with traceried fronts, and some have carved animals on the arms.

The east window consists of three lights and is filled with commemorative Victorian stained glass. There is older fifteenth-century stained glass in a north window, depicting the crucifixion. Beautiful delicate tracery ornaments the underneath of the communion rail, which may date from the fifteenth century. It once formed part of the screen in a church at nearby Booton. The remnants of a sedilia, in the form of two small arches, still survive over a window-sill.

Thorpe-next-Hadiscoe – St Matthias

Thorpe-next-Hadiscoe is situated about 4 miles north of Beccles and can be reached off the A143. The small church dates back to the Saxon period, but it was built on by the Normans. A reed thatched roof shelters the nave. It has a scalloped ridge with a thatched apron below, finishing with inverted scallops just above the eaves level. The chancel and south porch have slate roofs.

The lower part of the flint round tower is Saxon and the upper part Norman, except for the crenellated parapet, which was added in the fifteenth century. The lower part of the tower has several blocked slit windows. The top section has twin round-headed bell openings divided by central ornamented shafts. The flint-walled nave is basically Norman, with two thirteenth-century windows on the north side, one a lancet the other with Y-tracery. The south porch, which was added in the fourteenth century, has wave mouldings on its arch. Buttresses support the corners of its front gable wall. There is also a north doorway. The Victorians rebuilt the chancel with brick in 1838, with brick buttresses also supporting the walls. The pitch of the roof was lowered at the same time, no doubt to accommodate the use of slates; thatched roofs require much steeper pitches.

Inside is a square Norman font of Purbeck marble, each side of its bowl simply ornamented with shallow blank arcades. Four separate pillars surround the sturdy stem. The Victorians renewed the roof of the nave.

The west nave wall, by the tower arch, has an ancient double recess with pointed arches, perhaps once used for storage, as one side contains a shelf. The chancel has a memorial to Thomas London, who died at the age of twenty-one in 1661; there is a brass plate with a Latin inscription. The east window is of three lights.

Thurgarton – All Saints

Thurgarton is situated about 6 miles south-west of Cromer and 17 miles north of Norwich, about 4 miles west of the A140. All Saints stands in a solitary position in the countryside near a quiet crossroads, with several trees surrounding it. The Churches Conservation Trust now cares for it, after the church had fallen into a dilapidated state, during the second half of the twentieth century. It was declared redundant and in 1984–5 the Trust rethatched the nave, chancel and porch using reed, with the roofs furnished with straight ridges. They also renovated the building, as well as tending to the overgrown churchyard.

It is a fourteenth-century flint church. It stands tall and barn-like; even the porch has two storeys. It once had a west tower but it fell down in 1882. Some of the remains of the base were incorporated into a small vestry, which was constructed on the site of the tower in 1924. The thatched roof sheltering it, with a straight ridge, complements the thatch on the nave, chancel and porch. The vestry does not extend across the full width of the west wall, so the two single lancet windows in the nave have a westward view either side of it.

The church walls are buttressed; an unusual buttress supporting the south-east corner of the chancel, has a semi-arched passage through it. The chancel appears to have been shortened at some time during its history and a small priest's south door leads into it.

The light and airy interior of the church reveals a nineteenth-century timbered roof through which the underside of the thatch may be seen. There is a fascinating collection of fifteenth-century benches, with poppyhead ends and carvings of various figures, on each side of the aisle. The carvings include two dogs fighting, an elephant and castle or howdah, a winged griffin, musicians, and a grotesque human figure carrying a large club. The medieval octagonal font has a sturdy stem and an eighteenth-century cover rising to a point. The chancel screen dates to the nineteenth century and the east window is of three lights.

THURLTON – ALL SAINTS

Thurlton lies about 9 miles north-west of Lowestoft and can be reached off either the A146 or the A143. All Saints church stands in the village opposite the junior school. Separate thatched roofs cover the nave and the chancel, and a parapet wall divides the two surfaces. Points decorate the ridges and the chancel has a large thatched apron terminating in inverted scallops just above the eaves level.

The buttressed walls of this basically Norman church consist mainly of flint, as also does the large square west tower, which was built in the fifteenth century, when other construction work was being carried out on the church. The tower is unembattled and small areas of the walls reveal decorative work of knapped flints and stone. The louvred bell openings are round-headed and traceried.

The porch is located on the north side and has a statue niche over the entrance arch; the arch itself has carved shields in the spandrels. Patterns of flint, dressed stone and brick ornament the gable wall. The inner doorway is even more elaborate, with a square hood-mould and carved angels in the spandrels swinging censers, as a prayer rising to God. There are further angels in the mouldings, together with a series of crowns, many of which have been damaged. There is another doorway on the south side, which displays typical Norman motifs such as zigzags and billets.

The medieval octagonal font stands on a large similarly shaped pedestal. Lion statuettes support the stem while shields and roses decorate the bowl. A large fifteenth-century wall painting of St Christopher dominates the north wall. It is faded, but various aquatic creatures can still be discerned swimming at his feet, some large and others small. The screen dates from the fifteenth century and contains panel tracery over the one-light crocketed arches. The Victorian stained-glass leaded east window consists of three lights and depicts the nine orders of angels. The altar table below is small and plain. There are good memorials to two members of the local Denny family, one to Ann, who died in 1665, and the other to Margaret, who died in 1717. There is an arched alcove in the south chancel wall that may have once been a piscina.

In the churchyard stands the gravestone of Joseph Bexfield, engraved with the image of a Norfolk wherry. A wherryman, he drowned in August 1809 at the age of thirty-eight, leaving a widow and two children. Local folklore claims his ghost may still be seen wandering in the marshes, before vanishing into the river. He reputedly died because he ignored a warning not to cross the marshes at night because a will-o'-the-wisp, locally called the Lantern Man or Jack o' Lantern was there, luring people into peril with the light of his lantern. Flickering lights have often been reported darting from place to place over marshland at night. One possible explanation for the phenomenon may be the spontaneous ignition of marsh gas, or traces of acetylene rising from decaying vegetation.

THURNE – ST EDMUND

Thurne is situated about 12 miles east of Norwich, in the Broads, and may be reached off the A47. A reed thatched roof with a straight ridge covers both the nave and the chancel; a small parapet wall divides the two. The church is basically late thirteenth century, with inserted fifteenth- and sixteenth-century windows. The arched brace nave roof is also sixteenth century. A Victorian restoration took place in the early 1850s.

The unbuttressed square west tower was constructed mainly of flint in the late thirteenth or early fourteenth century and has three-stepped battlements that were added later. They are ornamented with flint and brick chequered patterns. The bell openings below are louvred and the belfry houses a fourteenth-century bell, cast in Norwich. The west wall of the tower has a lancet positioned directly above a circular window.

Buttresses support the nave walls, which are now mostly covered with rendering. A porch with a statue niche above the entrance shelters the north door and there is also a pointed-arched south doorway. A priest's door leads into the chancel, the walls of which are mainly of flint with a few brick courses laid above, reaching to the thatched eaves level. A cross perches on top of the east gable wall.

The interior of the church was much altered by the Victorians, who replaced the pews and the font, and installed new glass in the five chancel windows. They also replaced the glass in the south nave window with stained glass showing angels and medallions. However, they kept the fifteenth-century rood beam, the late seventeenth-century communion rail with dumb-bell-shaped balusters and an early seventeenth-century holy table. The chancel also retains a fourteenth-century trefoiled piscina.

THURTON – ST ETHELBERT

Thurton sits about halfway along the busy A146 road between Norwich and Beccles. St Ethelbert's church stands on a rise in a peaceful church-

St Ethelbert, Thurton, Norfolk

yard that is approached up a stony lane. The churchyard serves as a wildlife sanctuary and is kept as a refuge for wild flowers; there are over sixty species of flora.

A continuous thatched roof covers both the nave and the chancel, and spreads both north and south around a little square west tower. This gives the illusion that the embattled tower is grafted on to the timbers below the thatch. A thatch apron extends below, and scallops and points ornament the ridge. The brick and flint porch also has a thatched roof. The church was restored in 2005. The base of the tower has a fourteenth-century window but the top section, built of brick and flint, was added later, possibly in the early sixteenth century. The tower has louvred bell openings, large for its small size, with rounded heads.

The 900-year-old walls now have rendering to protect them. The church consists of a single-cell building, with early fourteenth-century windows. Brick buttresses support the north wall. An outstanding feature is the magnificent stone Norman south doorway, with its decorative mouldings and zigzag carvings on its four concentric arches. The brick-blocked Norman north doorway is not as elaborate but is stylistic. There is a good variety of stained glass, including medieval and seventeenth-century French glass, some of which possibly originated in Rouen. The latter is found in the three-light east window. Most of the stained glass was installed by

Norman doorway at St Ethelbert, Thurton, Norfolk

Samuel Yarrington in 1826, with some by Robert Allen. Allen's west tower stained-glass window shows eight saints placed in insets. The oldest glass is an early fifteenth-century English holy trinity, showing God the father, with a dove symbolizing the holy spirit and the crucified Son below.

There are also faded medieval wall paintings, including an elaborate late fifteenth-century or early sixteenth-century large St Christopher on the north wall, opposite the entrance. The saint bears the Christ child on his shoulder, with images of a lobster, crab and other aquatic creatures swimming in the water at his feet. There is another indistinct wall painting to the east of it that is difficult to interpret but is probably of the fourteenth century.

The plain octagonal font is thought to be of a seventeenth-century date. It has a slim wooden cover and stands on a wooden octagonal pedestal. The communion rails are also seventeenth century.

Thwaite St Mary – St Mary

This thatched church lies about 6 miles south-east of Norwich and is reached off the B1332. It is a low building comprising a Norman nave, a

St Mary, Thwaite St Mary, Norfolk

square west tower added in the fifteenth century and a chancel of the eighteenth century. The church and pretty churchyard are well cared for and a lantern lamppost stands near the doorway.

The reed thatched roof, with a neat straight ridge, covers the nave, but the chancel roof is tiled. The chancel walls are built of brick but rendering shields the nave walls. The tower is of flint but contains areas of brick, including a brick stair turret. It has no battlements or buttresses but the parapet has a narrow band of stone cog-like ornamentation. The louvred bell openings have tracery.

The outstanding feature of the church is the beautifully carved Norman south doorway, which has various motifs around its arches. The hood-mould has scallops around its arch, carved at right angles to the wall. To the left of the doorway on the south exterior wall, there are two unusual memorial plaques, one fixed each side of a nave window. The wide thatched eaves shelter them from the effects of the weather.

The interior is simple. Black and red tiles cover the floor. The font bowl is of uncertain date but the stem, with eight columns arranged around a bold central support, is thought to date from the fourteenth century. Opposite the south door there is a painting of the Virgin and

East window of St Mary, Thwaite St Mary, Norfolk

child. The Victorian stained-glass three-light east window, with elaborate tracery, also shows the Virgin and child in its central light. The other two lights have two roundels each, displaying the symbols of the four evangelists. The rest of the leaded windows are fitted with clear glass; there are no windows on the north side. The wooden chancel screen has trefoiled arches with no tracery and dates from the fourteenth century. The chancel has a blue painted wooden plank ceiling supported by intersecting wooden beams.

West Somerton – St Mary

West Somerton lies just over a mile from the North Sea and its exposed, windy location has resulted in the installation of some massive wind turbines next door to the ancient St Mary's church. It commands views of the sand dunes and the sea. It may be reached from the B1159, off the A149.

A thatched roof covers the eleventh-century nave and the fifteenth-century north porch but slates shelter the roof of the chancel, also of the fifteenth century. The thatch ridge has scallop ornamentation. Below the thatched eaves of the nave, the roof slope has been extended with tiles,

St Mary, West Somerton, Norfolk

which discharge rainwater into guttering. Thatched roofs normally do not need guttering, as the wide overhang of the eaves throws rainwater well clear of the walls.

The round tower, constructed of flints, dates back to the thirteenth century, but the octagonal section above was added later. A brick parapet tops the tower and probably dates from the sixteenth or seventeenth century. The tower contains four lancet bell openings, arranged on alternate surfaces of the octagonal belfry; the remaining four have been closed up with knapped flints. The belfry houses a fourteenth-century bell thought to be the earliest inscribed one in Norfolk. It was cast at King's Lynn. The small rectangular holes that are visible all over the tower walls were originally installed to secure the wooden scaffolding poles used during its construction. Many have since been filled to protect the tower masonry. The base of the tower has a two-light leaded west window that was installed in the fourteenth century. A small narrow window with a brick surround was placed higher above it.

As the tower originates from the thirteenth century and the nave the eleventh century, it is fairly certain that the original church had no tower. It might have fallen down very quickly, but there is no evidence of this. Both the nave and the chancel walls are built of flint rubble and knapped flints. Many of the windows display Y-tracery and are of the fourteenth century.

The east window of five lights was renewed during the Victorian restoration in 1867. Entry to the church is via the north door, the arch of which is thought to date from around 1300.

An interesting feature of the interior is the various fourteenth-century wall paintings that have been uncovered, buried beneath the whitewashed walls. Many are faint and severely damaged. On the south wall, a large painting of the last judgement is depicted but it is difficult to interpret because of its poor condition, with many parts obliterated. It originally showed Christ in majesty sitting on a rainbow, with angels each side of him, with the Virgin and St John interceding for those about to be judged. Below there are two angels sounding trumpets, with many figures stepping out of their tombs signifying the resurrection of the dead. There is also a St Christopher carrying the Christ child, unusually placed on the south wall near the door; his staff and hand are still visible. On the north wall a badly damaged painting depicts the passion scene and the resurrection. It includes the triumphal entry into Jerusalem, the mocking, the flagellation and the resurrection of Jesus, with him stepping out of the tomb, his hand raised in blessing.

The bowl of the octagonal font, which dates from the fourteenth century, is not ornamented. In contrast, the fifteenth-century pulpit pays tribute to the woodcarvers' skill. It is hexagonal and skilfully decorated with concave panels and tracery above their arches. Unusually positioned on the west wall is a set of the ten commandments; they were originally displayed on the east wall. The restored boards are thought to be of the sixteenth century, rather than the much more common ones of the Victorian period. The benches in the church are nineteenth century.

The chancel arch dates from the fifteenth century and the screen below is also of the same period. The screen dado has traceried panels and foliage, and the upper part has ogee arches and further fine tracery. The recess in the wall leading to the rood stairs has now been blocked. The sanctuary retains its ancient piscina but the altar is nineteenth century. The altar front, which was added later, commemorates the coronation of Queen Elizabeth II in 1953. The oak reredos was donated in 1912 in memory of the long-serving Revd Joseph Budd.

The somewhat unusual churchyard is almost completely treeless. The grave of Robert Hales, known as the Norfolk giant, may be found in the north-east corner of the churchyard. A farmer's son, born in 1820 at West Somerton, he grew to a height of 7 feet 8 inches, exceeding the height of Henry Blacker, known as the British giant, who was born in 1724, and reached the height of 7 feet 4 inches. Robert Hales was presented to Queen Victoria and appeared in many shows and fairs.

WOODBASTWICK – ST FABIAN AND ST SEBASTIAN

Woodbastwick lies about 8 miles north-east of Norwich and may be reached off the A1151. The thatched church lies near the village green, which has in its centre a picturesque thatched water well, the former village pump. Several thatched cottages, the old thatched vicarage and thatched barns also enhance the rustic beauty of the surroundings. A tiled lychgate leads into the churchyard.

The joint dedication to St Fabian and St Sebastian is unique in England; the two saints share the same feast, 20 January. Their symbols are displayed inside the church on the south wall; St Fabian's shows a blue shield bearing a silver dove with an olive branch, while St Sebastian's consists of a silver shield carrying three vertical red arrows.

Individual Norfolk reed thatched roofs cover the nave, chancel and porch of the flint-walled church. A parapet gable wall, with crow-steps on top divides the nave from the smaller chancel. The nave ridge and porch are both decorated with scallops, but a straight ridge tops the chancel thatch. Parts of the church date from the thirteenth and fourteenth centuries but a major restoration project took place in 1878–9, under the guidance of the renowned Victorian architect Sir George Gilbert Scott. He heightened the west square-buttressed tower with battlements and

St Fabian and St Sebastian, Woodbastwick, Norfolk

renewed the pinnacles at each corner. The tower has round-arched bell openings and a traceried west window. It also has a clock that was donated by the late John Cator to mark the millennium.

A statue of St Fabian, pope and martyr, with his staff, greets visitors over the porch. On the entrance door a notice states:

Enter this door
as if the floor within were
gold
and every wall of jewels
all of wealth untold.
As if a choir
in robes of fire
were singing here
Nor shout, nor rush,
but hush:
for God is here.

A nineteenth-century stone font with an oak cover in the shape of a spire stands inside the south door. The bowl is elaborately ornamented. A stoup can be found to the right of the south door and there is another on the south wall by the lectern. The interior walls bear several memorials, the one on the south wall in memory of the parishioners who lost their lives during the two world wars. The north wall carries three commemorative tablets to members of the Cator family, who were great benefactors of the church; one of them bore the cost of the restoration carried out by Sir George Gilbert Scott. The benches lining the central aisle have poppyheads at their ends. The needlepoint kneelers all have chevron patterns. At the top of the nave, there is a lozenge-shaped memorial to Ann Cator. Behind the pulpit, there is another to Elizabeth Margaret Cator, who was a bridesmaid to Queen Elizabeth, the Queen Mother. The memorial reads:

ELIZABETH MARGARET
Devoted wife of MICHAEL
CLAUDE HAMILTON BOWES LYON
Warm hearted courageous
and humble of spirit
she left behind for those who
knew and loved her a memory
infinitely precious and of
abiding worth
1900–1959

Statue niche at St Fabian and St Sebastian, Woodbastwick, Norfolk

Michael Claude Hamilton Bowes Lyon was the Queen Mother's brother.

The Victorians inserted the stained glass, except for one window in the vestry. However, the window tracery survived and dates to the fourteenth century or earlier. The glass in the south wall windows in the nave show various scenes from the life of Christ. The north windows pay homage to his miracles, such as the changing of water into wine at Cana. Another stained-glass window remembers John Cator, who died on 20 August 1858, aged seventy-six, and Elizabeth Louise Cator, who died on 11 February 1847, aged fifty-nine. The east window of three lights shows St Sebastian. He was a Roman soldier who was martyred by being pierced with arrows, but recovered. Later he was clubbed to death after confronting the emperor for his cruelty.

There is an altar in the small room to the left of the chancel; it was formerly a chapel but is now used as a vestry. The medieval wooden screen stands under the pointed chancel arch. A rood towers above the screen. The figure of Christ was carved from a single block of wood. In the sanctuary there is a piscina and the beautiful painted altarpiece pictures two saints on either side of the Virgin and child enthroned, with the magi bearing gifts.

Altarpiece at St Fabian and St Sebastian, Woodbastwick, Norfolk

WOODRISING – ST NICHOLAS

This tiny village is situated about 7 miles north-west of Attleborough and may be accessed north of the B1108. The church is normally locked but a key-holder lives across the road.

Unusually, the tower bell shelters under a thatched roof in the churchyard but the fourteenth-century church is not thatched. Half of the tower collapsed at some unknown date before 1742, although a forewarning of such a possibility was contained in a church record to the Bishop of Norwich, dated 1602, stating, 'The steeple is in very great decay.'

After the catastrophe, the heavy wooden bell frame was renovated and resited in the north-west of the churchyard. The tower rubble was left where it fell and became a mound. This has since shrunk, but a small heap still survives covered with ivy. The Norfolk reed hipped thatched roof, reaching low to the ground, shields the bell frame. The thatch has a raised straight ridge, ornamented with cross-rods and liggers. Wire-netting protects the thatch surface and trees now encroach around the structure. The thatch eaves terminate just above ground level but there is enough room when kneeling to view the wooden frame and its suspended heavy single bell. The bell was cast by George Mears of Whitechapel in 1861 and

Thatched bell frame at St Nicholas, Woodrising, Norfolk

is still rung when a service is held. It is triggered by a bell pull on the ground outside the housing and the sound echoes through the small gap between the eaves and the ground. The bell ringer once used to crawl below the thatched eaves and sat inside to ring the bell.

NORTHAMPTONSHIRE

Horton – Chapel of St Francis of Assisi and Our Lady Queen of Heaven

This is a private Roman Catholic chapel in the Menagerie Gardens at Horton. The delightful gardens date from the eighteenth century. The Menagerie is located 5 miles south-east of Northampton and visitors enter from a signposted field gate off the B526 Northampton to Newport Pagnell road. A short journey follows along a single-track road across an open field, passing over a cattle grid. Parking is available by the wicket gate at the end of the track. There is a charge for entry into the gardens; the opening dates are April to September, Monday and Thursday only, between 2 p.m. and 5 p.m. Teas are available in the garden.

Chapel of St Francis of Assisi and Our Lady Queen of Heaven, Horton, Northamptonshire

In 1756, Lord Halifax, who lived at Horton Hall, built the Menagerie in his park as a folly. At the same time he built two other follies, one a triumphal arch and the other a thatched temple in the form of a neo-Classical arbour, with an Ionic portico, frieze and pediment. The Menagerie now serves as the main house on the estate, as Horton Hall was demolished in the 1930s. The thatched temple was recently converted into the Roman Catholic chapel. There is also another thatched arbour in the garden but this was built later and it is now used privately by the family.

The whole estate became neglected, until Gervase Jackson-Stops acquired it in 1975. By that time the Menagerie house had become derelict. Jackson-Stops was an architectural historian and architectural adviser to the National Trust, and he initiated a restoration programme. At the same time he used the classical temple as his outdoor dining room. Vernon Russell-Smith designed the rose gardens in 1989. Since then the property has changed hands and the new owner has carried out further developments. He was responsible for the main restoration of the beautiful gardens that took place in 1992–4, to a design by Ian Kirby. He also converted the classical temple into the Roman Catholic chapel, and it was consecrated in 2002. The family now use it as their private chapel for regular worship. A brass plate on the front gives the following details:

Chapel of St Francis of Assisi
and
Our Lady Queen of Heaven
Blessed on 25 May 2002
by Abbot Geoffrey Scott OSB
assisted by
Dom. Alexander Austen OSB
Canon T. Cronin
and
Fr. R. Creighton-Tobe CO.

It is circular and domed, with its formal façade overlooking a formal pool. A statue of Christ adorns the front pediment. The rest of the chapel has a rustic aspect, enhanced by its circular, undulating domed straw thatched roof. Tall plants also enclose the shady retreat.

Unlike the formal stone front, the rest of the walls are constructed of simple oak boles. The rear has a rustic neo-Classical design. Tree columns

Oak bole walls of Chapel of St Francis of Assisi and Our Lady Queen of Heaven, Horton, Northamptonshire

Rustic rear exterior of Chapel of St Francis of Assisi and Our Lady Queen of Heaven, Horton, Northamptonshire

support it and a statue of St Francis of Assisi stands on the back pediment. The north door is made of bamboo.

Inside, a series of stars sparkles on the ceiling. There is also a bronze of Our Lady Queen of Heaven specially made for the chapel by Mother Concordia Scott OSB, of Minster Abbey. The whole concept is very atmospheric. In addition to the main path leading to the formal front of the chapel, there is a more secret secluded serpentine path starting at the rear, which gives access through the gardens to the main house.

The curious name, the Menagerie, dates back to the eighteenth century when, as I have said, it formed part of the estate of Horton Hall. At that time there was also a moated area in the park to confine different species of animals that were kept on display, in case they escaped from their cages. Thomas Wright of Durham designed the whole concept of the park around 1770. He was a garden designer, architect and astronomer. In the latter field, he was the first to discover that the Milky Way was composed of stars. The blue ceiling of the chapel, with gold stars, therefore represents Heaven. It may be of interest that before Michelangelo painted the ceiling of the Sistine Chapel in the Vatican, it was also painted blue with stars representing Heaven.

OXFORDSHIRE

WROXTON – ST THOMAS OF CANTERBURY

This thatched Roman Catholic church is located in Silver Street, in Wroxton, which lies on the A422 Banbury to Stratford-upon-Avon road. It is best reached from junction 11 of the M40. The church is well worth visiting for its unusual collection of stained-glass windows. Trinity College holds the lease of the land on which the church stands, but it is part of St Joseph's in Banbury.

The little church, which was erected in 1894 by the Hon. Mrs. Benyon, is plain and rectangular. Later, in 1948, it was entirely reconstructed and restored during the ministry of Canon A. G. Wall. The present thatched roof over the gabled church has a plain flush ridge of straw, with two tiny eyebrow windows peeping through the thatch on each side of the roof slope. A wooden slatted bell tower rises over the ridge at the entrance gable end, facing the roadside. Just below the bell tower there is a statue of St Thomas of Canterbury high on the gable wall, sheltered by a small wooden canopy above.

Below, a small gabled porch, roofed with stone tiles, is flanked by two stained-glass windows that are also sheltered by individual gabled roofs.

St Thomas of Canterbury, Wroxton, Oxfordshire

In addition, there are four stained-glass windows on each side of the building and a further three behind the altar, the central one of the trio being larger than the others. Small dripstones protect all the windows on the outside of the church, the walls of which are of a roughcast finish.

The stained-glass windows are a unique collection, the ones each side of the entrance being the only original ones. They can be viewed from inside by opening the two doors that lead into the small rooms that hide them from view. They depict the occupations of the locals, as relevant today as they were 100 years ago. Sheep shearers, sowers and reapers are portrayed. Proverbs are also incorporated into the glass, such as 'He that tilleth his land shall have plenty of bread' and 'Wheat is not gathered in the blade but in the ear.' Others include: 'Industry is fortune's right hand and frugality her left' and 'A scabbed sheep will mar the whole flock.'

The three windows behind the altar at the east end of the church, together with the eight side windows were all salvaged from other churches that were destroyed by bombing in the Second World War. The church leaflet explains that their seemingly random theme is due to this, and also explains the unusual fact that the three windows behind the altar all depict the transfiguration of Christ. The other side windows show

Stained glass window in St Thomas of Canterbury, Wroxton, Oxfordshire

Towards the chancel of St Thomas of Canterbury, Wroxton, Oxfordshire

various biblical scenes, such as the last supper, the betrayal of Judas kissing Christ, Jesus on the way to Calvary and Christ carrying the cross.

The doors of the church are Gothic in design, constructed of wooden planks, and the wooden trestle benches each side of the aisle are plain. The cross sits high inside the church on one of the horizontal roof timbers, with the Virgin standing on the right and St John on the left. Other statues include the Madonna and the sacred heart. The stations of the cross may be found around the walls of the church.

The early history of the Catholic Church in Wroxton is interesting. It is indirectly linked to the famous Wroxton Abbey, a ruined Augustinian priory founded by Michael Belet, in honour of St Mary, in 1207. This is situated further down the sloping main street from St Thomas's church. A fine gabled house was built on the site of the ruined priory in the seventeenth century. Later Lord North, who was the British Prime Minister during the time of the American War of Independence, purchased the property. In 1841, one of his descendants, the Baroness Susan North, married a Catholic named Doyle, who eventually became the new Lord North after a special Act of Parliament was passed. He arranged for Catholic services to be held in the abbey chapel, but later they were transferred to a mission at the North Arms public house. However, in 1887 he founded a small chapel in Wroxton and dedicated it to St Thomas of

Canterbury, so that the village could have its own permanent site for Catholic worship.

SHROPSHIRE

LITTLE STRETTON – ALL SAINTS

Little Stretton lies off the A49, about 2 miles south of Church Stretton. The church is opposite the Ragleth Inn at the north end of the charming village street. It is a very attractive building, despite being an imitation of an earlier form of half-timbered Gothic architecture.

It was built in 1903 as a chapel of ease, and was used for the first time when a service was held on 20 October of that year. Mrs Alice Elizabeth Gibbon of the nearby Manor House, which dates from 1600, paid for its construction. She had also been responsible at an earlier date for the construction of another church at All Stretton, the third of the three Strettons. A plaque on the wall inside the church pays a tribute to her:

All Saints, Little Stretton, Shropshire

'For more than 30 years she devoted her life to the people of Little Stretton. Beloved in the village she carried comfort and happiness wherever she went and her life was an inspiration to all who knew her.'

In 1958 the Church Commissioners purchased the church for the benefit of the parish of Church Stretton. It now forms part of the united parish of St Laurence's, Church Stretton, with St Michael's, All Stretton, and All Saints, Little Stretton.

It was unusual for churches to be built with thatched roofs at the beginning of the twentieth century. All Saints was first erected only as a temporary structure from a prefabricated kit supplied by a Manchester ironmonger. However, it became permanent and extensive alterations and decorations were made soon afterwards. Its galvanized iron roof was replaced with thatched heather, owing to the excessive noise created when it rained on the original tin roof. Heather was once quite widely used for thatching. It was harvested during autumn when still flowering and laid to dry with its roots uppermost before use. It probably came from the nearby Long Mynd plateau where it grew profusely. The plateau rises to about 1,700 feet and spreads over thousands of acres. It stretches, north to south, for about 10 miles and is administered by the National Trust.

The church was thatched again in 1935 and on several occasions afterwards. In 2005 it was rethatched in water reed, with a straw ridge. As is usual with a straw ridge, it was covered with wire netting to protect it from bird damage. A series of small thatched gable windows peep through the main expanse of thatch, and a pretty wooden bell tower rises on the ridge, with a cross on top.

The outside walls of the half-timbered church are painted a mixture of black and white; as is usual the vertical and horizontal timbers are black and the panels between are white. The colour scheme blends naturally with the rest of the village, where old cottages of similar colours abound. The white doors and windows are in Gothic form; the latter are leaded lights.

A small wooden porch leads into the church, and inside all the walls and the A-shaped ceiling are of wood, as well as the supporting roof beams. The walls and ceiling are lined with tongue-and-groove planks of pitched pine. The wooden open bench seats are of the trestle type and the lectern is crafted from wood. Alice Gibbon's two sons presented the wooden font in memory of her in 1933; it is octagonal and copper lined. Even the organ is of wood; it was installed in August 1967 to replace a harmonium that had previously been used since 1917.

Wooden interior of All Saints, Little Stretton, Shropshire

Wooden font of All Saints, Little Stretton, Shropshire

Outside a picturesque garden surrounds the church, with laburnum, lilac, roses and well cared for flower-beds. There is also a sundial given as a memorial to a former parishioner. The beautiful churchyard and garden bring back memories of the short poem 'God's Garden' by Dorothy Gurney:

The kiss of the sun for pardon,
The song of the birds for mirth,
One is nearer God's Heart in a garden
Than anywhere else on earth.

SOMERSET

Portishead – Friends Meeting House

This thatched Quaker meeting house is located at 11 St Mary's Road in Portishead, near Bristol. It is best reached off the A369 Portishead to Clevedon road.

The meeting house, with its small burial ground, is Grade 2 listed. It dates from about 1669 and was possibly built on land occupied at that time

Friends Meeting House, Portishead, Somerset

by Thomas Hodds. He had earlier met George Fox, the founder of the Society of Friends, when he visited Portishead. It is also possible that it may have been a conversion of the thatched cottage that Hodds lived in. William Prowse owned the land on which it stood and donated it to the Quakers. The basis of Quaker life and practice is the conviction that there is something of God's spirit in everyone and that every soul can have communication with God, without the need for an intermediary. Their meetings start in silence and anyone, when moved, can utter brief passages of prayer or ministry. Quakers therefore do not rely on priests, clergy or leaders.

The meeting house has a wheat reed roof topped with a plain flush ridge, and is wire-netted to prevent bird and wind damage. A stone parapet wall at the rear gable end protects the thatch gable edges from the weather, but the front gable edges are left exposed. Over its long history, the building has obviously been rethatched many times, the latest in 2005. The walls consist of whitewashed stone rubble; previously they had been pink. In recent years, a porch with a side entrance was erected on the front gable wall, which also carries a square chimney, with a small window slit below. Another small room with a lean-to roof has also been added. Both

Front gable wall of Friends Meeting House, Portishead, Somerset

extensions have natural stone finishes, only the original building being whitewashed.

The exterior is plain and unassuming, as were most other Nonconformist chapels at the time. This was because of the persecution and imprisonment of those who rejected the established church by attending so-called illegal meetings. In 1683, during the reign of Charles II, the persecution reached fury pitch. In order not to attract the attention of the authorities and also in keeping with their beliefs, Nonconformist buildings were deliberately made simple, a form of architectural camouflage. However, Quakers were more reluctant to hide away than other Nonconformists and simply chose plain buildings without pomp and ceremony. The situation eased after the passing of the Toleration Act in 1689, which enabled Friends and other dissenters to worship without hindrance and to register places of worship for their own use. However, Quakers still encountered some hostility because of their refusal to pay tithes.

Portishead's meeting house consists of a simple square room, with wooden benches arranged around a central table, although most early meeting houses originally had a raised platform with benches opposite the entrance, as this offered a convenient way of seating those with a gift for ministry. Although Quakers have no ordained clergy those with a gift for ministry are encouraged to use it. Later, all benches faced forward, with women sitting on the left and men on the right. Windows were usually placed quite high in the walls to reduce outside distractions that might interfere with devotion. From the early twentieth century, many Quaker meeting houses started to divide rooms for various purposes. They often installed movable wooden panels fitted on slide tracks or used hinged concertina type panels that could be opened or closed. They were sometimes used to separate the sexes by creating two separate rooms.

Tivington – St Leonard's Chapel

Tivington lies in the extreme north of the county, near Minehead, and about 1½ miles south-east of Selworthy. It is best reached off the A39. St Leonard's stands by the roadside. Parking is difficult, because of the narrowness of the road, but the chapel is left open for visitors. Entry is by the west door.

This chapel of ease was built around 1350 by Sir Ralph de Midelney,

St Leonard's Chapel, Tivington, Somerset

who represented Somerset in parliament and was a knight of the shire. It under a wooded hill in rural surroundings. Its roof consists of combed wheat reed and the thatch extends and shelters the cottage that is built on to the east end. Thatched tufts ornament the ends of the flush ridge, which also has two parallel liggers with spars. The National Trust, which owns the adjoining cottage and the surrounding Holnicote Estate, now cares for the chapel, and has done so since 7 July 2002. Occasional services are still held there.

The thick walls of the single-cell chapel are built of stone rubble with a lovely reddish hue. A large, wide-based chimney rises up the side of the north wall, making an interesting exterior feature. The chapel has just three windows, one in the western end of the north nave wall and one each side of the chancel. They are of stone, straight-headed with two lights; two have cusps but the one in the south chancel wall does not. They are small, leaded with square clear glass panes, with a few light green ones interspersed. Hood-moulds shield them.

The west chapel door has attractive linenfold panelling and above there is a bell in an open wooden housing, located under the thatch eaves. It is reputed to have come from a yacht called the *Lady of St Kilda*, which belonged to a member of the Acland family, who were great benefactors of the chapel. They formerly owned the Holnicote Estate before the

Bell and west door at St Leonard's Chapel, Tivington, Somerset

National Trust took it into its care after Sir Richard Acland, the 15th baronet generously gave it to them in 1944.

There is a history of the chapel on display, which relates that it ceased to be used for worship after the Reformation. At that time, it also had a straight-headed east window that was blocked when the cottage was built on to the east wall. It then had several other uses, including a store, a barn and, during the nineteenth century, a dame's school. The latter was the name for a small primary school in the eighteenth and nineteenth centuries run by a female teacher for the benefit of local poor children. It was eventually used for religious services again in 1896, owing mainly to the efforts of the local Acland family, one of whom later gave it to the Church.

Repairs were carried out in 1940. A member of the Acland family was responsible for the panelled reader's desk, which was made out of parts of an eighteenth-century box pew that originally stood in the parish church. The family also gave the plain, straight oak benches that came from Milverton church, near Taunton. They probably date from the middle of the nineteenth century. Local parishioners made the colourful hand-embroidered kneelers. Wooden parquet tiles cover the nave floor and the

Open fireplace inside St Leonard's Chapel, Tivington, Somerset

walls are whitewashed. The ceiling consists of white planks behind timber beams. The large open fireplace in the nave makes an unusual feature, it has a wooden bressummer. A small charming devotional piece of the Madonna and child sits on the mantelpiece.

The altar rail is wooden and flagstones cover the chancel floor. A lovely donated triptych stands above the altar. The centre panel shows the nativity with the magi bringing gifts, with their horses and entourage in the

Triptych in St Leonard's Chapel, Tivington, Somerset

right background. The left door depicts St John the Baptist, with the Lamb of God and the right door shows St Christopher carrying the Christ child across the river. The triptych, reputedly Italian, bears more resemblance to northern Renaissance art and may be a copy of such. The altar hides a door built in the dividing wall of the adjacent cottage, the sitting room of which is used as the vestry.

SUFFOLK

Ashby – St Mary

This thatched church lies 5 miles north-west of Lowestoft and about 3 miles north of Somerleyton. It is located in a wild, remote area in the middle of a field; there is no village. Several rough tracks lead to it; the one from Lound is just passable for cars and is known locally as Snake Lane. However, it is possibly best approached on foot.

Both the nave and the chancel are thatched with water reed and the ridge is decorated with a series of points. There are early records showing that the Victorians rethatched the chancel in 1893 and the nave was rethatched in 1929. The roofs have obviously received attention several times since. Like many old thatched cottages, simple branches cut from trees form some of the underside timbers supporting the thatched roof.

The bottom third of the round tower was built by the Normans or possibly the late Saxons. The other two-thirds, in octagonal form constructed on top, is probably sixteenth century. The octagonal section was laid on the round walls using angled brick quoins. The top, with battlements at each corner of the octagon, was added much later. Each face of the octagonal tower has a lancet widow set within a brick surround. The total height of the tower is about 50 feet and a fan-vaulted roof sits on top.

Both the nave and the chancel are probably thirteenth century. There are no porches and the flint walls are unsupported by buttresses. A scratch dial may be seen in the jamb of the south door; there was once also a north door but it is now blocked. Clear glass is used in the windows, some of which are of the lancet type, possibly of thirteenth-century origin, in the chancel.

Steps lead down into the church. The former sanctus bell window above the tower door is now blocked. The bell was rung at the consecration of the host before the Reformation. The font is also probably thirteenth century; it is made of Purbeck marble supported on a central stem, with five additional wooden pillar supports that were added in the fifteenth century. The arched piscina in the south wall is also thought to be thirteenth century and beside it there is a lower sedilia. A Victorian restoration replaced both the benches and the choir stalls. The choir stalls that were introduced are constructed of oak and have poppyheads, whilst the simple movable benches in the nave have open backs.

A memorial stone stands by the churchyard gate, honouring the memory of American airmen who crashed nearby during the Second World War. Some belonged to the 100th Bomb Group, nicknamed the 'Bloody Hundreds'.

Barnby – St John the Baptist

This church lies about 6 miles west of Lowestoft, on the opposite side of the A146 to Barnby village. The square embattled flint tower probably dates to the early fourteenth century; no buttresses support it. The Decorated west window in the tower suggests it is of the same period. The main body of the church is thought to be twelfth or early thirteenth century.

St John the Baptist, Barnby, Suffolk

A reed thatch roof covers both the chancel and the nave. The ridge of the roof, decorated with points and liggers with cross-rods, is new compared with the rest of the thatch. Both roof slopes have ornamental aprons below the ridge. The remains of a scratch dial are still visible in the middle of the flint south wall. Many windows contain coloured glass in their leaded lights, with Y-tracery. However, there are some stained glass ones, with roundels set in them. The east window is stained glass. One window in the north-east side of the chancel has been blocked. The north door of the church has also been blocked. The south porch has rendered walls, with a tiled roof.

The interior of the church conceals a rare banner stave locker, still in place to the west of the south door. Its rarity lies in its medieval door, elaborately decorated with tracery piercing and primitive scratch work. Such lockers were used for storing the staves that carried the processional banners. The faded remains of some fifteenth-century wall paintings also still survive on the south wall. These depict the crucifixion and the works of mercy growing on a tree. The original six works of mercy show Charity tending the hungry, the thirsty, the stranger, the naked, the sick and the prisoner. A further painting on the south wall, in its traditional position opposite the entrance, is that of St Christopher, the patron saint of travellers. The octagonal font is of Purbeck marble.

Barsham – The Most Holy Trinity

This large church lies about 3 miles south-west of Beccles and may be reached off the A145 or the B1062. Entry to the churchyard is through a thatched lychgate, with a timber support for its roof. It was constructed in 1893 but new gates were installed in 1997.

The nave of the church is thatched, but tiles cover the chancel and porch. There is a round tower and a most outstanding and unique east gable wall.

The reed thatched roof has good ornamentation; points decorate the ridge, with two thatched aprons directly below. The first apron finishes with a series of points, with some inverted scallop shapes between them. The second ends near the eaves with a series of small inverted scallops. A fire broke out in 1979 that completely destroyed the nave roof. Many of the timbers had to be replaced and the thatch was renewed in 1982,with a similar decoration to that on the original roof. Incidentally, the burning thatch that fell into the nave during the fire also caused some damage to

The Most Holy Trinity, Barsham, Suffolk

the box pews that had replaced the originals, which were removed in 1870. A few scorch and burn marks are visible on some of the poppyhead finials.

The lower part of the round tower, constructed of flint cobbles, probably dates to the twelfth century, with an inserted fourteenth-century west window. The part above the level of the thatched ridge was probably also added in the fourteenth century. The belfry stage above contains five bells and is sixteenth century.

The east gable wall and window form the outstanding feature of the church. A huge diagonal trellis of stone completely covers the exterior flint and stone wall and also the large stained-glass east window. From inside the church, the trellis appears as window tracery. Experts disagree on the date it was constructed, but recent opinion suggests it is most likely to be the middle of the fifteenth century. Interestingly, the Etchingham family were the lords of the manor of Barsham from 1420 to the 1540s and their heraldic shield contains a near identical trellis to that covering the east wall.

The nave and chancel are thought to be mainly fourteenth century, although the chancel was greatly restored in 1870. There are two aisles and a lady chapel. The church has had a long association with the Suckling family and Admiral Horatio Nelson. In the north-west corner of the chapel, there is a memorial tablet to Catherine Suckling, wife of

Thatched lychgate of The Most Holy Trinity, Barsham, Suffolk

Towards the east interior of The Most Holy Trinity, Barsham, Suffolk

Edmund Nelson and mother of Horatio. The north-west central window in the nave was installed in 1905 to commemorate the anniversary of the Battle of Trafalgar, fought on 21 October 1805. It was dedicated to the Suckling family, a member of whom served under Nelson aboard HMS *Victory*.

The pulpit in the nave is Jacobean, with a sounding board added later; some of the lower panels were damaged in the 1979 fire and replaced in 1981. By the pulpit steps, a fragment of a rare example of a 1636 communion rail may be seen; there are only two other dated examples surviving in England. The early fifteenth-century font stands on the base of a previous one, which dated back to about 1150 and is now kept in the sanctuary. Storm damage necessitated a restoration of the sanctuary in 1905.

In 1547, it was ordered that all rood lofts must be taken down. The present rood screen, erected in 1893, has on the top the crucifixion with the Virgin Mary to the left, and St John the Evangelist to the right. The base of the screen is painted with colourful green and red panels. The arch over the screen was painted and decorated in memory of the church patron and benefactor, the Revd Robert Alfred John Suckling, in 1919.

The communion rail donated by a Miss Fairbrother in 1895 has its top inlaid with ebony and inscribed with, 'My flesh is meat indeed' and 'My blood is drink indeed.' The church organ dates back to 1875. In 2005, a Trafalgar bicentennial commemoration project was launched to carry out a complete restoration of the organ. When finished, it is hoped that the new keyboard will be made of oak that was on HMS *Victory* at the Battle of Trafalgar.

Bramfield – St Andrew

This church is located 9 miles west of Southwold on the A144, south of Halesworth. The most striking exterior feature is the Norman flint round tower that stands several feet away from the main body of the church. It is unique, being the only detached round tower in Suffolk. It was probably originally built for defensive purposes; its massive walls measure about 5 feet thick and the height approaches 44 feet. It contains five bells and the top has a small brick embattlement, with some brickwork around the bell openings.

Reed thatch covers both the nave and the chancel of the nearby church and a parapet wall divides the two surfaces. The attractive roofs have thatched aprons below the ridges, finished with a series of points. Points also decorate the ridges. There is guttering below the eaves for rainwater,

St Andrew, Bramfield, Suffolk

Separate tower at St Andrew, Bramfield, Suffolk

which is unusual for a thatched roof. The high pitch of the roof and the wide eaves of the thatch are designed to throw water well clear of the walls to keep them dry. In contrast, the low-pitched porch roof has a bituminous covering and the lychgate leading to it is tiled.

The church dates to the fourteenth century and the original cross remains on the west gable. The interior walls are painted cream. The nave windows are part of a Victorian restoration and have floral decorations with surrounding edges of light green glass. Each flower represents a religious symbol. The lily in the north wall window symbolizes purity, the Virgin Mary and the immaculate conception, whilst the olive in the other north window represents peace. The south wall window has the passion flower with the five stamens representing the five stigmata, the marks left on Christ's body by the nails and spear at his crucifixion. The other south window contains the rose, symbolizing the sinlessness of the Virgin Mary, the rose without thorns. The stained-glass windows in the chancel are dedicated to Nicholas and Elizabeth Simons, who carried out the Victorian restoration of the church. The reredos was installed early in the twentieth century.

The magnificent rood screen, with one-light divisions, elaborately carved and with painted panels, was made in the fifteenth century. These medieval paintings on the base of the screen show St Mark and St

Rood screen of St Andrew, Bramfield, Suffolk

Matthew towards the north side, while the south side depicts St Luke, St John and Mary Magdalene. On the north wall of the nave a faded fifteenth-century wall painting survives. It shows a white cross and four angels with outspread wings in each corner, offering the holy cup to the cross. Other figures of angels are depicted below.

Sir Edward Coke, who owned the neighbouring manor of Huntingfield in the latter part of the sixteenth and early seventeenth centuries, became Lord Chief Justice of England. His son and daughter-in-law, Arthur and Elizabeth, who died in the 1620s, are remembered in the form of an exquisite effigy. Elizabeth holds a baby in her arms, with her husband kneeling in full armour. The effigy was made by Nicholas Stone, a renowned sculptor of Renaissance art, who also did work in Westminster Abbey.

There are also many memorial floor slabs. One ledger slab describes the life and death of Bridgett Applewhaite. It reads:

After the Fatigues of a Married Life,
Born by her with Incredible Patience,
For four Years and three Quarters, baring three Weeks;
And after the enjoiment of the Glorious Freedom
Of an Early and Umblemisht Windowhood,
For four Years and Upwards,
She Resolved to run the Risk of a Second Marriage-Bed
But DEATH forbad the Banns.

It continues that fate in the form of apoplexy intervened and she collapsed in the arms of her husband-to-be and died soon after in 1737, aged 44 years.

Another floor slab commemorates the Rabett family who lived in nearby Bramfield Hall, in the sixteenth and following centuries. Four of their coats of arms have hung in St Andrew's since the eighteenth century. The rabbits that ornament their painted shields are probably a play on the family name. The benches with poppyhead finials are a replacement for the box pews that were removed in the 1860s and 1870s restoration. Flowers, butterflies and birds, depicting the wildlife of the Suffolk countryside, decorate the box kneelers; the work was done by the present generation of worshippers.

Bures – St Stephen's Chapel

Bures is about 6 miles south-east of Sudbury, off the B1508. The chapel lies about a mile north-east of the town. It is best reached by travelling up

St Stephen's Chapel, Bures, Suffolk

Bures High Street and proceeding straight up Cuckoo Hill, to a farm building, now used as a furniture factory workshop, on the right-hand side of the road. A key-holder may be found there. From the workshop, follow the track that leads to the chapel.

It stands on the site where, according to tradition, the Coronation of King Edmund took place on Christmas Day, 855. In 1218, Cardinal Stephen Langton consecrated the chapel, following its construction on the site. After the Reformation, it fell into disuse and was used only as a barn. Incidentally, the local people still call it Chapel Barn. It was not until the 1930s that a local resident, Isabel Badcock, with her brother-in-law Will Probet, restored it. When the work was completed, it was rededicated to St Stephen. A brass memorial to Isabel Badcock can be found on the north wall inside the chapel. She died on 27 August 1939 and her memorial states that she 'took joy in the restoration of this chapel'.

A reed thatched roof covers both the chancel and the nave. The ridge is furnished with scallops and points and the roof has a decorative thatched apron below, ending with a series of inverted points. The walls of the church vary in type: the chancel consists of flint rubble, the nave of weatherboarding and the vestry of brick, with some timber-framing above with herring-bone brick infilling.

Entry to the chapel is through a north door that leads into the vestry

The De Vere Monuments, St Stephen's Chapel, Bures, Suffolk

and then through an arch into the nave. It is very dark inside, with a wooden ceiling. It is lit only by candles as there is no electricity. The De Vere monuments that nearly fill the aisle further enhance the eerie atmosphere. They were formerly at Colne Priory, now disused, at Earls Colne, in Essex. Two of the effigies on the tomb chest lie side by side in the centre of the aisle. One is of Richard de Vere, the 11th Earl of Oxford, who died in 1417, and the other of his wife Alice (Sergeaux). Another monument in the aisle is of Thomas de Vere, the 8th Earl of Oxford, who died in 1371. A further monument to the north-west is of Robert de Vere, 5th Earl of Oxford, who died in 1296.

The chapel contains several lancet windows, with some stained glass. The ancient stained glass in the three stepped lancet east window depicts various images: St Stephen heads one, the middle one shows Christ in majesty, and the third St Laurence. A large wooden crucifix stands in front of the stone altar. The altar rail is also of stone, with a wooden top. A piscina is set in the south wall of the sanctuary and opposite, in the north wall, there is an aumbry for the holy vessels. The north wall of the nave has a gallery. There are four wall paintings in the nave, two on the north wall and two on the south; there is also a consecration cross. They are painted in red or russet colours. Tiles cover both the nave and chancel floors.

Consecration cross in St Stephen's Chapel, Bures, Suffolk

BUTLEY – ST JOHN THE BAPTIST

Butley is situated about 12 miles north-east of Ipswich on the B1084. The church stands by the roadside and dates from the Norman period. A beautiful thatched roof covers the nave, with its ridge decorated with closely cut scallops and points. Tiles cloak the chancel roof which dates from around 1300. The church is normally left open.

The square west tower is castellated and flushwork ornaments the battlements. The bell openings below have Y-tracery. The south porch, built of red brick in the sixteenth century, is interesting because the thirteenth-century hood-mould over the entrance arch must have been salvaged from a former building or porch. A statue niche lies empty above the arch. The porch has a tiled floor and the inner south doorway offers a moulded Norman arch with zigzags. The doorway has been altered; it was once moved to another location and later returned to its original position. The north doorway has also undergone change.

The octagonal font is ornamented with angels and lions, and the benches on each side of the aisle are plain. The screen spans the full width of the church; there is no chancel arch. The doorway in the north wall formerly led to the rood loft. The screen, which possibly dates from the fifteenth century, has one-light divisions, with ogee arches above, and the dado is plain and solid. The door on the south side is the priest's door.

Coney Weston – St Mary

Coney Weston lies about 11 miles north-east of Bury St Edmunds, from where it can be reached via the A143 and B1111 roads. An unusual sign-post on a small green shows a colourful picture of Coney Weston's fourteenth-century thatched parish church. However, the church is actually outside the village, about a mile to the east on the road to Hopton.

It stands back from the road and consists of a chancel and a nave, with buttressed walls and a porch on the south side. The tower fell down in 1690, damaging the west wall, which was rebuilt using the debris of flint and limestone from the fallen tower. Thatch now only covers the nave; the porch and chancel are both tiled. The ridge of the thatch has scallop ornamentation. The chancel was once also thatched, but the roof fell into a dilapidated state and was replaced in 1891 by red tiles.

A notice inside the church informs visitors that 'the nave roof has always been thatched and was last thatched in 1960 by John and "Roper" Reeve, the famous thatching brothers from East Harling. In 1993, Rod

St Mary, Coney Weston, Suffolk

Moore renewed the sedge ridge and the condition of the main thatch is a tribute to the skills of the Reeves and the durability of Norfolk reed.' It is believed that the hidden timbers supporting the thatch are those of the original fourteenth-century truss.

The nave and chancel walls consist mainly of knapped flints, with some cobbles. The outside south chancel wall shelters a low arched recess, where formerly a tomb would have lain. The large, impressive porch, also of flints and cobbles, has a castellated parapet that supports a cross, and above there is a tiny bell-cote housing a single bell. The windows in the porch are traceried, as are the other plain glass leaded-light widows of the church. The faint image of a scratch dial is just discernible to the left of the porch. The hole that formerly housed the gnomon is more clearly visible that the actual dial.

St Mary's is a single-aisle church, with benches each side and a plain ceiling above. A notice gives the information that 'the church organ was made by "Father Willis" of Bristol and was installed in 1886 in the chancel but was moved into the nave in 1890'. Its wooden pump handle still remains. Nearby, the panels of the fourteenth-century octagonal stone font have carved floral decorations of roses and leaves. The lid is twentieth century. Some wall paintings on the north wall have been discovered hidden under a limewash. Restoration work suggests they are medieval in origin, owing to their reddish colour, but they appear to have been overpainted in black and white, with various Victorian texts. The church leaflet suggests there may have been other murals on the nave walls, such as the judgement of solomon, St Christopher and a stork with a serpent.

The chancel arch, behind the nineteenth-century pulpit, has two cusped arches to the left and also two shorter ones to the right. Both are fourteenth century. Those on the left contain paintings of the Ten Commandments and those to the right angels. The present altar was constructed from an old rood screen and contains paintings of various saints with their attributes. The two on the north side are thought to be of St Edmund and St Peter, the two to the south St Hugh of Lincoln and St Apollonia. The front of the altar pictures St Barbara, the Virgin Mary, St Barnabas, St John the Evangelist, St Margaret and St Ethelreda. Behind the altar may be seen in bold capitals, 'I AM THE BREAD OF LIFE.'

Original fourteenth-century tiles once covered the chancel floor but were moved to the north-west corner of the nave to protect them from wear. They are at present covered with carpet, as the corner is now used as the vestry. The chancel piscina, in the south-east corner, also dates from

Chancel arch in St Mary, Coney Weston, Suffolk

Angel under cusped arch at St Mary, Coney Weston, Suffolk

Altar pictures in St Mary, Coney Weston, Suffolk

the fourteenth century and has a quatrefoil basin. The remains of a very large and tall niche may be found to the left of it, placed in a corner angle. To the right of the piscina may be seen two steps that once formed part of a sedilia, where the priests would have sat before the chancel floor was raised in the nineteenth century. Finally, there is an old iron churchwarden's stave for catching and removing stray dogs from the church!

COVEHITHE – ST ANDREW

This church is situated about 7 miles south of Lowestoft, east of the A12 and 5 miles north-east of Southwold. It is a remarkable sight: a small thatched church built inside the huge roofless ruins of a magnificent Perpendicular English church, constructed in the late fourteenth or early fifteenth century. Only the square tower, with its ring of five bells and the tall, long, gaunt walls of the former church survive. Sea breezes now blow through the empty window spaces. The Churches Conservation Trust cares for the tower and ruins, and has done so since 1974. For many centuries the tower has been used as a landmark for shipping along the coast. An old legend suggests that a ghost haunts the ruins of the churchyard; she walks about at night, dressed all in white, and has no face.

Side view of St Andrew through ruins, Covehithe, Suffolk

Gable view through ruins of St Andrew, Covehithe, Suffolk

There are only a few houses nearby, but even when the ruined church was first built, the population of Covehithe numbered less than three hundred; a number out of all proportion to the size and magnificence of the church. It was financed by wealthy donation. Remnants of tracery, corbel heads, flushwork chequer-board panelling and pier mouldings hint at the excellence of this seven-bay church, with its separate chancel bay. John Sell Cotman, the artist who was a leading member of the Norwich School in the nineteenth century, did various depictions of the ruins. The East Anglian gentry employed him as a drawing master but he became better known for his landscapes and etchings. Many thought that Cromwell's forces were responsible for the desecration of St Andrew's but it appears that although they broke the stained-glass windows and destroyed several pictures within the church, they left the structure. About thirty years later it became obvious that the church was much too large and expensive to maintain, especially in view of the small population it served, and in 1672, the ecclesiastical authorities gave permission to erect the present smaller thatched church with material obtained from dismantled parts of the original church structure.

The tiny reed thatched church that arose within the ruins is still used for regular Sunday services. Scallops and points decorate its ridge. Some parts of the walls are stone but the north wall is built of brick. The porch has a red brick gable, with the head of an old bearded king inserted in it. There is also a niche or stoup in the west wall of the porch, and tiles cover the roof.

It is a light single cell church, with a traceried east window; all the windows are leaded lights. Plain wooden pews line the aisle and the three poppyhead pew ends at the west end came from the old ruined church. The pews stand on a wooden floor. The lectern, pulpit and prayer desk are all wooden but stand on a flagstone floor. The pulpit came from the ruined church, together with the octagonal font, which was slightly defaced during the Civil War. The bowl shows carvings of the four winged symbols of the evangelists – St Matthew's man, St Mark's lion, St Luke's ox and St John's eagle – together with four angels with musical instruments. The stem bears four lions.

There are two memorial stones set in the interior walls of the church, one in the south and one in the opposite wall. One commemorates Enoch Girling and the other James Gilbert; both are dated 1672, the year the tiny church was built.

Henstead – St Mary

St Mary's lies about 6 miles south-west of Lowestoft and about 2 miles north of Wrentham. It stands on a minor road linking the A12 to the B1127, its churchyard spanning both sides of the road. A well-cared-for thatched roof shelters both the nave and the chancel. Its ridge is decorated with scallops and points, with a long thatched apron below, ending near the eaves level with inverted scallop shapes.

The church is Norman, but in 1641 a fire spread from a nearby farmhouse on the eastern side and caused considerable damage. It burnt the carved benches, the interior woodwork and much of the chancel, and also destroyed a wooden chest that contained the parish 'writings'. The church was renovated, and later the Victorians carried out further restoration. More recent work, completed in the twentieth century, included the installation of the massive beam spanning the church bearing the cross in the chancel. Before the restoration that took place in 1906, the church had box pews and a three-decker pulpit.

A square, tall tower, constructed with knapped flints in the fifteenth century, dominates the west of the church. It is embattled and contains a single bell. The church walls, including the front of the south porch, are also built of knapped flints. Tiles cover the porch roof. The south

St Mary, Henstead, Suffolk

doorway leading into the church has a relatively unchanged Norman arch, with fine columns, one of which is spiral fluted. The arch formed above the columns shows concentric circles ornamented with various carvings, including zigzag work or chevrons. The north doorway arch is less impressive, with its one column and single chevron ornamentation.

One window in the chancel contains stained glass, as does the west window, which also has quatrefoil tracery. The south window consists of plain glass panes, and those to the north and east of clear leaded lights with tracery. A tall wooden cover, ornamented with a spire with the dove of the holy spirit on the top, sits on the modern font. The south-west corner of the nave contains a tall banner stave locker. Panelling decorates the sides of the chancel and the altar rail is made of pierced wood.

South doorway of St Mary, Henstead, Suffolk

St Mary's font, Henstead, Suffolk

HERRINGFLEET – ST MARGARET

Herringfleet is about 5 miles north-west of Lowestoft on the B1074. The church stands in a quiet position beside the road. Parking is possible outside the church, which except for Sundays is normally kept locked, but a key-holder lives nearby. A cobbled flint wall surrounds the churchyard.

A reed thatched roof covers the nave and porch, but the chancel, which stands at a lower level than the nave, is tiled. Points decorate the nave and porch ridges, with wide thatched aprons extending below, terminating in inverted scallops just above the eaves level. The Saxon flint round tower was built in the early eleventh century and stood alone, probably as a weapon store and for defensive purposes. Later, the Normans built the chancel, which was used as a separate wayside chapel. Later again, the Normans constructed the nave to join the separated sections together to form an integrated church structure.

The lancet windows in the tower are original and there are also bell openings above with rounded heads; each has a central column dividing the openings into two. The walls of the nave are built with flint and rendering protects them. Bricks now block the north doorway. The lancet window in the north wall of the chancel is the only Norman one. The rest in the chancel and nave are later, consisting of two-light leaded windows with tracery, some with clear glass and others with stained glass.

The south doorway into the church is Norman and chevrons ornament its arch. St Mary's has a west gallery, parts of which are made from the traceried upper section of the former rood screen. The pews have poppy-head ends. The outstanding feature of the church is the collection of early nineteenth-century stained glass installed in the east window. The pieces were reputedly brought back from a Franciscan friary in Cologne by Henry Mussenden Leathes, who visited the German city after taking part in Wellington's victory at Waterloo. Interestingly, the church has a monument to one of his ancestors, John Leathes who died in 1787. The Leathes were an old-established Herringfleet family.

ICKLINGHAM – ALL SAINTS

This church is located about 8 miles north-west of Bury St Edmunds, on the A1101 road to Mildenhall. The Churches Conservation Trust now cares for it.

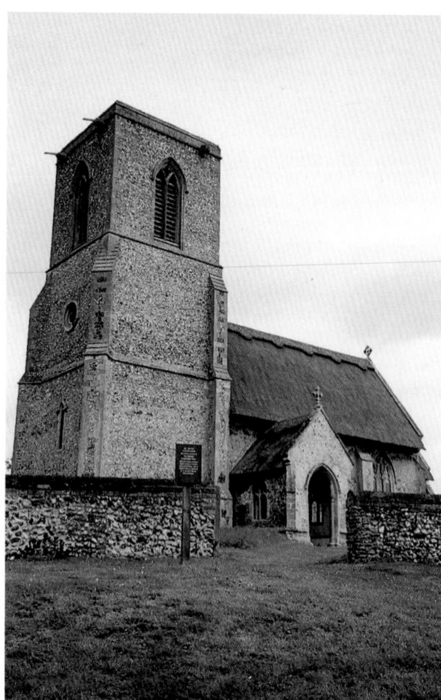

All Saints, Icklingham, Suffolk

It dates back mainly to the late thirteenth and early fourteenth centuries. However, the walls of the nave are twelfth century and there are blocked windows in the north wall. The church became redundant in 1972 but remains a consecrated building. It also remains unspoilt, having escaped any drastic restoration. It is surrounded by a wall, has a large green in front and stands on the highest ground in the village. A key-holder lives nearby.

Separate Norfolk reed thatched roofs shelter the nave, the chancel and the porch. Scallop shapes decorate the ridges, ornamented with cross-rods and liggers. Sections of the under-surface of the thatch remain visible inside the church and to enhance its attractiveness some parallel bands of matting have neatly patterned interwoven reeds, whilst adjacent ones have carefully aligned reeds.

The walls are constructed of local flints. The large square tower has gargoyles and louvred openings on each side. There is also a quatrefoil window on the west side. The tower adjoins the nave and contains three bells, their dates ranging from the fifteenth to the early seventeenth century. The nave has an elegant south aisle with octagonal piers and beautifully carved cornices, and some fine sculptural carving decorates the niches, either side of the aisle's east window.

Both the nave and the chancel are from the Decorated period. Only the lower part of the fifteenth-century rood screen still survives. The stained-glass windows generally date from the fourteenth century and some old glass is also found in the tracery. The octagonal font, supported on five columns, also comes from this period. Each side bears a different elaborate design and motif, a tribute to the mason's skill. The pulpit is seventeenth century. A remarkable array of fourteenth-century encaustic tiles covers the floor of the chancel and sanctuary. The tiles reveal an interesting variety of mosaic patterns, depicting birds, a lion's face, human faces and other images.

A seventeenth-century box pew stands just inside the south door but some of the benches in the nave date from the fifteenth century. Some are made of chestnut planks and others of oak, with ornamental poppyheads at each end. These are carved in the shape of fleur-de-lis, a common motif for bench ends. Many of the benches are backless, but a few have plain backs. At the west end, there is an interesting sixteenth-century chest, made of oak with fancy scrollwork. It was formerly used to store the churchwardens' accounts, the church plate and other valuable items. An ancient stone coffin rests in the north-west corner of the church with a carved cross on the lid.

Interior of All Saints, Icklingham, Suffolk

Iken – St Botolph

Iken lies 16 miles north-east of Ipswich and may be reached by turning off the B1069, about 2 miles south of Snape. The church stands on a knoll called Iken Cliff in an isolated position by the River Alde, overlooking the wide expanse of the estuary and salt marshes. The delightful situation caused one former incumbent, the Revd Arnold Wainewright, to remain for fifty-five years. His tombstone lies in the churchyard, which is set amongst a grove of trees. It appears very likely that St Botolph, to whom the church is dedicated, founded a monastery at Iken in 654, later destroyed by the invading Danes. He became one of the early founders of Benedictine monasticism in England. St Botolph, also known as Botulf, has sixty-four churches dedicated to him.

The church at Iken has a thirteenth-century nave thatched with reed, with its ridge decorated with scallops and points. The chancel fell slowly into a ruinous state after the Reformation, until the Victorians demolished and rebuilt it around the middle of the nineteenth century. Unfortunately, a devastating fire broke out in 1968, caused by sparks from a bonfire igniting the thatch on the nave roof. The isolated location of the church meant considerable delay before any help could arrive; it was then too late and the church was gutted, especially the nave. A drastic restoration lasting many years, eventually took place.

The knapped flint west tower, dating to the fifteenth century, escaped the worst effects of the fire. It has diagonal buttresses and battlements, all decorated with flushwork. The early sixteenth-century porch leading into the nave has similar ornamentation and the top of its gable wall consists of brick, topped with a tiled roof. Tiles also shelter the restored chancel roof.

The interior walls of the nave remain exposed and blackened from the fire. A statue niche is set in a wall. The fifteenth-century octagonal font survived the blaze; its squat stem is decorated with lion supports. The symbols of the four evangelists ornament the outside of the bowl, together with four angels displaying instruments of the passion, such as the lance, nails and whip. Near the font, the lower part of a heavy stone Saxon cross is displayed in a wooden cradle. Dr Stanley West discovered it built into the tower structure during the preliminary restoration work carried out in 1977. It may date from the ninth century, and is heavily decorated with carved patterns.

Ixworth Thorpe – All Saints

This small church is situated about 8 miles north-east of Bury St Edmunds. It lies just south of Ixworth Thorpe village, when travelling on the A1088, via the A143 from Bury St Edmunds. A flint and rubble wall surrounds the churchyard and the attractive entrance gate has entwined roses on a support over it. Although it is normally locked, a key-holder may be found during office hours at the farm just along the road on the opposite side to the church.

A wire-netted reed thatch shelters both the nave and the chancel, and the ridge, with cross-rods, has scallops ornamented with curved liggers and spars. The church has a gabled east end, with a weatherboarded bell turret supported on a substantial brick base at the west end. A large Tudor brick porch on the south side has a stepped gable with a small pyramidal roof covered with tiles. Interesting mixtures of flints in various motifs decorate the top of the porch above the doorway, just below the castellation.

The church walls are rendered and there is a Norman doorway in the south wall. Although plain, the doorway is tiny, only about 3 feet wide and just over 5 feet high to the springing of its arch. The windows consist of plain glass leaded lights with hood-moulds; those in the chancel are lancets whilst in the nave are a few Decorated period windows.

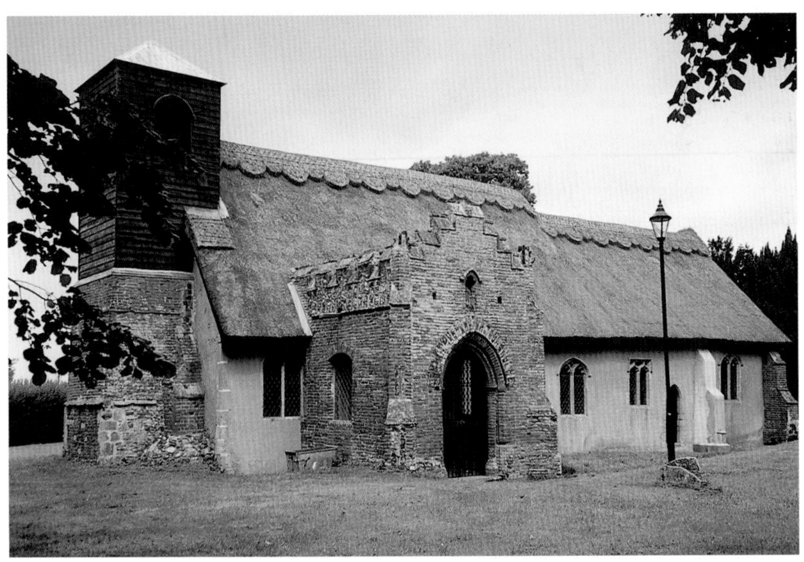

All Saints, Ixworth Thorpe, Suffolk

The benches arranged each side of the central aisle have poppyhead ends. They also have a wide range of different carvings on the arms. One depicts a thatcher with a thatching comb, a tool used to tidy thatch by downward combing. Others depict a variety of different images of animals, including a horse and a hare. Also shown are mythical creatures, such as a unicorn and a mermaid holding a mirror in her right hand. There is also an owl and a lady walking with a dog on a lead. The church contains an array of needlepoint kneelers with a variety of embroidered Christian symbols. A well-preserved copy of a 'Degree of Marriage', printed in 1771, has been stored in the church for many years.

The pulpit was installed during the Jacobean period and the three-sided communion rail dates back to the late seventeenth century. The churchyard, which is bordered by trees, sadly contains several children's graves, including that of a three-year-old, who also lost two brothers. The grave of a sixteen-year-old rests close-by.

Kessingland – St Edmund

Kessingland is situated about 4 miles south of Lowestoft just to the east of the A12. It lies very close to the sea and the tower of the church has served as a landmark to generations of mariners. The local lifeboat crew members are renowned for the hundreds of lives they have saved since 1869, when records were started. The North Sea has encroached on to the land and in the past swept away part of the village. The church is normally locked, except for the summer months when it is opened during weekday afternoons. It is fringed with yew trees. It once belonged to St Clare's Nunnery in London.

A reed thatched roof shelters the nave, with scallops and points closely cut on the ridge. The tiled roof of the chancel is separated from the thatch by a small parapet. Richard Russell of Dunwich built the lofty, square west tower, in the first half of the fifteenth century. He also designed the one at Walberswick, near Southwold. Diagonal buttresses ornamented with flush-work support the three-stage structure. A small brick top was added in the late seventeenth century, with gargoyles below. The tower has an impressive west doorway with a well-decorated arch; a seated figure of St Edmund dominates the middle of the frieze over the doorway. A three-light west window with tracery looks out immediately over the doorway, flanked by two large statue niches. The bell openings in the belfry are divided into three by two columns. In the late nineteenth century the belfry housed five bells.

St Edmund's once claimed a fourteenth-century south aisle but it was demolished in the sixteenth century and significant parts of the ruined walls remain in the churchyard. The filled-in arcade and octagonal piers can still be seen in the nave. In the seventeenth century, the north wall started to collapse and the nave was rebuilt in 1694. The octagonal font dates to the fourteenth century and is reputed to be one of Suffolk's finest. There are carvings of figures, including St Edmund and other saints on the octagonal stem as well as on the bowl; those in the former are standing whilst those on the latter are seated. The stained-glass east window was installed in the twentieth century.

Lindsey – St James's Chapel

This thirteenth-century chapel is privately owned, although English Heritage now maintains it. It is located on an unclassified road, ½ mile east of Rose Green on the outskirts of Lindsey and 8 miles east of Sudbury. Signposts point to it; it lies hidden within a small enclosure behind a roadside gate, next to a private residence. Entrance is free and it is open all year during daylight hours. It is no longer a consecrated building.

St James's Chapel, Lindsey, Suffolk

An English Heritage notice by the front gate states that the chapel dates from the thirteenth century and served two main purposes: it ministered to the adjacent Lindsey Castle, which was abandoned by 1400, only the earthworks remaining; and it served as a chantry where a priest would pray for the soul of the founder, a common medieval practice. A local family, Neste de Cockfield, instigated a tax to pay for its upkeep. However, all chantries and 'free' chapels were closed in 1547. The one at Lindsey became a barn and remained such until 1930 when it was restored.

It is thought that the roof may have been tiled before the fifteenth century, when it was thatched. The present roof consists of Norfolk reed with a sedge ridge ornamented with small scallops and cross-rod patterns. The thatch lies on a simple single-framed structure, secured to plates along the top of the walls.

The walls of the church are of flints, with simple lancet windows. There is also a three-light widow on the east gabled wall, above which the wall is clad with weatherboarding. The earliest parts of the chapel are the south wall and the north-east corner, both dating from the thirteenth century. The two lancet windows in the south wall are also of this date but

Piscina inside St James's Chapel, Lindsey, Suffolk

are of different heights. The piscina on the south wall is the original thirteenth-century one; it has a slightly cusped head and two trefoil-shaped basins. The south doorway has an interior arch. The interior appears gloomy because of the small size of the windows.

North Cove – St Botolph

This church is located about three miles east of Beccles and can be reached off the A146. It is situated next to the Three Horseshoes public house.

Its unbuttressed west tower, built with red bricks and flints, has a simple square shape. The bricks that form the quoins are possibly of Roman origin. The top of the tower is crenellated and louvres cover the bell openings. The church dates back to the early thirteenth century. The walls are mainly of flint, and brick supported by buttresses.

A reed thatched roof shelters both the nave and the chancel in one continuous, long sweep, with no parapet wall dividing them. Scallops and points decorate the ridge and a thatched apron lies below it, on the south slope only. This apron is similar to those on other thatched churches in the neighbourhood, suggesting that the same thatcher has cared for them.

The south porch was added in the fourteenth century and tiles cover its

St Botolph, North Cove, Suffolk

roof. A cross stands on the top of its gabled wall. It contains two attractive stained-glass windows, one in the west and the other in the east wall. Both consist of two lights, with quatrefoils above. There is a cross carved into the moulding of the Norman south doorway, which has chevrons on its arch.

There is no chancel arch, but there is a Victorian screen. The stained-glass windows are attractive and those in the chancel have quatrefoils; the Victorians inserted them during their restoration of the chancel. The octagonal font comes from the fifteenth century, with four lions and four angels ornamenting it. On the nave wall, some seventeenth-century texts were uncovered during restoration work in the 1930s.

The most remarkable feature of the church must be the number of large fourteenth-century wall paintings that were discovered in the chancel, all on the life of Christ. The north wall has scenes from the passion and the resurrection, coloured in red and yellow hues. A separate painting on the same wall depicts the harrowing of Hell or descent into limbo. The south wall shows Christ in judgement, displaying the wounds that were inflicted on the cross. A nearby painting is of the ascension, with the apostles staring in awe as Christ rises up towards heaven.

Pakefield – All Saints and St Margaret

This large church overlooks the sea directly on the front at Pakefield, on the southern outskirts of Lowestoft, on the A12. A war memorial stands just outside by the roadside. It is most unusual because it was once two separate churches, built side by side and separated by a common interior wall. They served two parishes, each with its own rector, but shared not only the same divided building, but also the churchyard. Only the southernmost of the two has a west bell tower; the east walls ended with a double gable, as the churches were joined lengthways.

After the Black Death, which devastated the population in the second half of the fourteenth century, the churches were combined for a time by knocking a series of seven arches with octagonal piers through the solid wall. When the population recovered, the arches were blocked off, converting the building back into two separate churches. However, in the middle of the eighteenth century it was decided to breach again the long interior wall separating them by opening up the arches that had been closed off. In effect, this left the joined churches with two naves, seven bays and a chancel. The need for two rectors then ceased.

All Saints and St Margaret, Pakefield, Suffolk

During the Second World War the church was severely damaged, when two incendiary bombs scored a direct hit in 1941. The burning thatch that fell into the church devastated the interior. After extensive repairs were completed it was reconsecrated in 1950.

The square flint tower dates from the fourteenth century. It is embattled but not buttressed, and louvres protect its bell openings. The reed thatched roof runs continuously over the full length, stretching west to east. A neat straight ridge adorns the top. Owing to the double gable structure, in an M-shape, there are in effect four thatched surfaces in the double saddleback roof; one to the north, one to the south and two meeting over the centre, discharging their rainwater into a shared central gutter. The south porch also has a thatched roof. There is a niche to the right of it set into its exterior wall, which was used as a stoup for the holy water. An old sundial can also be seen directly over the centre of the porch.

The church is mainly of flint, with some brick, and many parts still date back to the fourteenth century. The two east windows are also of this period. Most of the other windows consist of clear glass leaded lights, with the odd one containing a little stained-glass inset in its centre. Four angels, two lions and two white harts decorate the bowl of the octagonal font. Since the white hart, as a symbol, owes its origin to King Richard II, the font may date from the late fourteenth or early fifteenth century. A further four lions ornament the stem of the font. The oldest brasses in the church are of the early fifteenth century.

The churchyard stretches over a large area, and despite the presence of cottages and houses around three sides of it, the size makes it peaceful. Unfortunately, it is normally locked. For many years, the village stocks stood outside one of the churchyard gates.

Ringsfield – All Saints

Ringsfield is about 3 miles south-west of Beccles and can be reached off the A145 or from the B1062.

The square unbuttressed flint tower of the church was probably begun around 1450 but the present parapet dates from the seventeenth century. The top of the tower has brick and flint ornamentation. The church itself was probably built in the fifteenth century but the extensive restoration work carried out by Butterfield in 1883 destroyed most of the evidence of its precise origin. The chancel was completely rebuilt at that time.

All Saints, Ringsfield, Suffolk

The chancel, nave and north porch, which contains a lancet window, are thatched with reed, with a thatched apron ending just above the eaves. The roof was rethatched in 1953 and has been patched several times since. Local thatcher, James Ball, replaced the ridge, which is decorated with points, in 2003 and also did some work on the main roof slope. The rainwater from the roof discharges into wide guttering. The Tudor south porch, which gives entry to the church, is constructed of brick and dates from the sixteenth century. Its crow-stepped gable is a reminder of the Dutch influence in East Anglia. The roof of the porch is tiled.

A large seventeenth-century monument to Nicholas Garneys, who died in 1628, is built into the recess of a brick surround on the outside of the eastern end of the south wall. It bears an inscription with a pediment above. On the outside north wall, in a corner beside the thatched porch, there is an elaborate marble monument erected in 1902 to Princess Caroline Murat, the granddaughter of Napoleon's sister. She married twice, her second husband being the owner of Redisham Hall. The monument depicts a large angel pointing with one hand towards Heaven. A large cross lies in a horizontal position at her feet. Two other angels kneel facing her, on each side of the foot of the cross. Sanders of

The Garneys monument, All Saints, Ringsfield, Suffolk

The Murat Angel monument, All Saints, Ringsfield, Suffolk

London sculptured the monument, which is known as the Angel Monument.

Inside the church, the fifteenth-century octagonal font has carvings on its bowl and stem of various figures, including angels, flowers and lions. The half-screen, the pulpit with its sounding board and the bench ends are late sixteenth or early seventeenth century. The benches have straight edges to their tops but others along the central aisle have knobs.

In more recent times, a robin built a nest in a most unusual place – the lectern inside the church. It was left undisturbed so that she could rear her family there. Some time later, the old lectern was replaced with a new one, but the robin was not forgotten and the new one was carved with an image of a robin. Another picture of a robin, made in metal, can also be seen on the gates of the south porch.

Rushmere – St Michael

This church is located about 6 miles south of Lowestoft; the village is signposted a short distance to the west of the A12 and the church lies just outside, to the north. It is on a slight rise, in a relatively isolated position. Interestingly,

St Michael, Rushmere, Suffolk

most churches named after St Michael are by ancient tradition found on hill-tops. There is a round tower constructed of flint cobbles which may be of Saxon origin. It has late thirteenth-century bell openings displaying tracery.

Reed thatch covers both the chancel and the nave, both of which have flint walls. The chancel is slightly wider than the nave, which is a little unusual. The ridge of the thatch is decorated with scallops and points, with a thatched apron below on one roof slope only. The apron design bears similarities to that on the nearby church at Henstead, suggesting that the same thatcher worked on both. The underside of the thatch may be seen from inside. The church itself appears well cared for, although the churchyard has been left to grow wild.

The red tiled roof of the late seventeenth-century red brick porch shelters an attractive moulded doorway. The tall stone niche to the right of the door may once have been used as a banner stave locker. The small niche nearby, complete with bowl, was obviously once used as a stoup. A thirteenth-century priest's door can be seen and also two scratch dials.

The font inside the church dates from the fifteenth century; four angels and flowers decorate the bowl and four lions ornament the stem. An ancient faded wall painting still survives in a window recess. The pulpit has Jacobean panels and there is a small piscina set in the jamb of the south-east window of the chancel.

South Cove – St Lawrence

The small church at South Cove can be found on the B1127, about four miles north of Southwold. It lies by marshland; it is interesting that most churches dedicated to St Lawrence are built on or near marshland, for reasons that remain a mystery. Both the nave and the chancel are thatched with water reed, with a scallop and pointed ridge. The south slope was rethatched in 1950, with reed donated by Sir Robert Gooch, cut from the marshland on his Benacre estate. A local thatcher carried out the work. The cost of the thatching, complete with its wire-netting came to the sum of £50. In 1993, the whole roof was rethatched but by this time the cost had risen to the region of £17,000. A slate roof shelters the porch, which was built in 1880.

The church has a square west tower, built with knapped flints in the fourteenth century. Diagonal buttresses, decorated with flushwork, support the embattled structure, which contains one bell. The bell openings have wooden criss-cross trellis and there is also a leaded-light window in the east wall.

The narrow, thick-walled nave of the church is Saxon, from about 1000; the original high arched doorways have had later, lower Norman door arches inserted into them. The south one has some zigzag carving around

St Lawrence, South Cove, Suffolk

its arch. Just inside, a stone slab on the floor is believed to cover a crusader grave. A scratch dial has been set in the outside wall of this doorway. The door in the north doorway is fifteenth century, but that in the south doorway is later. Restoration of the nave's arched brace roof, with its wooden ceiling, took place from 1993 onwards. There is a single aisle, with most of the floor laid in brick. However, around the pulpit and lectern is new oak flooring. Pews with poppyhead ends line each side of the aisle. Many are Victorian replacements but there are some of the fifteenth century.

The thirteenth-century octagonal font has been defaced. It may have been retrieved from another ruined church, where it had been exposed to weathering. The bowl carries the winged symbols of the four evangelists: St Matthew's man, St Mark's lion, St Luke's ox and St John's eagle. Three angels and a shield are also depicted. The font has a wooden cover and stands on a pedestal made of rubble and ancient plaster.

The pulpit has wood carvings and nearby in the north wall may be seen a rare long, narrow, painted rood screen door that led to the former rood loft, dating from about 1470. The large painting that adorns it is of St Michael the archangel. Unfortunately, it is rather worn and faded. Parts of the original rood screen also survive.

Pulpit and rood loft door in St Lawrence, South Cove, Suffolk

Directly opposite the painted door, a stoup has been set in the interior south wall. The windows in the chancel and nave date back to the Early English architectural period, but much of the glass had been replaced. Most are clear glass leaded lights, with margins of coloured glass. However, the east window contains stained-glass leaded lights. The thirteenth-century sanctuary has an original piscina, with a sedilia. The reredos is wooden.

THEBERTON – ST PETER

This flint and stone church lies on the B1122 about 7 miles north of Aldeburgh. Many Australians visit it because of the village's connection with a suburb of Adelaide, which was named after it but incorrectly spelt Thebarton. Colonel William Light, the Surveyor-General, was empowered to select the site of Adelaide and thus was the founder and planner of the city. He once lived at Theberton Hall during his childhood, with the Doughty family. Charles Doughty, who was born there in 1843, was the author of *Travels in Arabia Deserta*, published in 1888. Residents of Theberton and Adelaide have over the years made generous contributions toward repairs to the church. The village and Adelaide were officially 'twinned' in 1984.

St Peter, Theberton, Suffolk

St Peter's is a long church with a light interior. Norfolk reed thatch shelters both the chancel and the nave. The total length of the thatch is about 100 feet, and scallops and points ornament the ridge. The roof was last rethatched in 1973, by local thatchers Rackman and Son. Three large animal gargoyles drain the roof, an unusual phenomenon for a thatched one, as rainwater is usually cast off the eaves directly to the ground. The base of the round flint west tower is Norman but an interesting feature is that at a point level with the ridge of the thatch, an octagonal belfry was added in about 1300 and the top was later embattled during the fifteenth century. The battlements are decorated with flushwork, a mixture of flint and dressed stone. The belfry contains six bells and the bell openings contain Y-tracery. The two-light west window in the tower is a fifteenth-century insertion.

The nave and parts of the chancel are also Norman; a continuous plaster ceiling covers both, but the old timbers supporting the roof are still visible at the tops of the walls. The south porch, opposite the vestry, was built in about 1470; above the entrance is a niche, with the crossed keys of St Peter and the crossed swords of St Paul in the spandrels. Inside there is no chancel arch. However, a colourful three-bay arcade, with painted octagonal piers, and arches above, divides the nave from the south aisle, known as the Doughty Chapel, which contains memorials to the Doughty family. The Victorian organ is painted white, with pipes in red and green. A

The arcade of St Peter, Theberton, Suffolk

Norman arch, dating from the early twelfth century and considered one of the best in England, stands on the inside of the vestry. It is carved with two orders of zigzags.

Both the hexagonal pulpit and the octagonal stone font date from the fifteenth century. The bowl of the latter is carved with lions and angels bearing shields, displaying the emblems of the trinity. On the stem there are also lions, angels and the wild, hairy men with clubs known as 'wodewoses'. In the sanctuary, an aumbry with its original wooden medieval door is set in the north wall. There is another aumbry, in the form of a niche, in the southern side of the east wall. A piscina stands beside the sedilia in the south wall. The stained glass window above the altar depicts the resurrection.

On the north side of the nave, a stained-glass window installed in 1917 commemorates Lt Col Doughty-Wylie, who won a posthumous Victoria Cross at Gallipoli, in the First World War. A further reminder of the war are the fragments of a German Zeppelin brought down nearby, during an air raid in 1917, which are exhibited in the porch. Some of the crew were buried in the churchyard extension, which caused some local controversy at the time. In the 1970s, their remains were removed to a German cemetery in Staffordshire. A war memorial commemorating the dead of the two world wars stands beside the churchyard gate.

St Peter's font, Theberton, Suffolk

THORNHAM PARVA – ST MARY

This small, isolated church, which dates from Norman times, lies in a spacious churchyard with many trees. It is much visited because it is the home of a famous medieval retable, considered one of the finest examples of English pre-Reformation art. St Mary's lies off the A140, about 3 miles to the west of Eye. A car park is conveniently situated at the front of the churchyard. The church is usually left unlocked because an alarm system protects it.

Thatch covers the whole of the church, including the unbuttressed square west tower, with its pyramidal steeple. The use of thatch on the latter is a rare feature. It presents a formidable task to the thatcher, who has to lay the thatch bundles at steadily changing angles to follow the configuration of the four-sided steeple. On a pyramid, only the central bundles on each face can be laid vertically and in line with the main pitch of the roof. The last time the church and tower were rethatched was in 1978. Ted and Paul Watlings, thatchers from nearby Worlingworth, carried out the work on the nave and chancel with Norfolk reed, together with some coarser Scottish water reed on the nave. Specialist thatcher Richard Clark was brought in to thatch the steeple. The straw ridge is ornamented with scallops and points.

St Mary, Thornham Parva, Suffolk

The walls of the church consist of local flints. Both the north and south doorways date from the Norman period; the north one is plainer than the south, which has shafts, scalloped capitals and roll moulding.

Inside the nave, both the north and south walls have faded early fourteenth-century wall paintings. The ones over the north door depict the story of St Edmund, Anglo-Saxon king of East Anglia and martyr, who was killed by the invading Danes in 869. One painting shows his vain attempt to flee from them. After capture the legend suggests that they tied him to a tree and scourged him before shooting him with a multitude of arrows. He was then beheaded and his head hidden in a bush. A wolf later discovered it and lay down to guard it until his followers retrieved it. One of the paintings shows the wolf. The monks then reunited the holy head with the body. A painting depicts this scene too, and another shows Benedictine monks bearing his coffin. The paintings on the south wall represent the birth and early years of Christ. They include the visitation, the nativity, the annunciation, the adoration of the magi and the presentation in the temple. All the wall paintings were restored in the 1980s.

The south window by the door contains medieval glass, with two inset engraved Lawrence Whistler roundels as a memorial to Lady Osla Henniker-Major. The pulpit is seventeenth century and above it can be seen two sawn-off beams, the remains of a medieval rood loft. The octagonal

Chancel screen and retable at St Mary, Thornham Parva, Suffolk

stone font dates from the early fourteenth century. The west wall supports a Georgian bow-fronted gallery, where musicians would have once played. The small circular window above the gallery dates from the late Saxon period. The charming kneelers are unusual; they are embroidered with scenes depicting different types of Suffolk house. The oak wooden screen, with one-light divisions, is early fifteenth century but the chancel is of the Decorated period.

The church's prize possession is the famous fourteenth-century retable; expert opinions suggest it was probably painted around 1330 in East Anglia. It is one of the very few that survived the destruction of the English Reformation, probably because it was closeted at that time in a Roman Catholic family's private chapel, at Stradbroke, in Suffolk. It then disappeared from sight until it was rediscovered by chance in 1927, in the stable loft of nearby Thornham Hall, owned by Lord Henniker. He donated it to St Mary's and therefore saved it for posterity. It is now placed behind the altar. It was painted and gilded on a panel of oak constructed from a series of vertical planks, with carved arcades fitted on the front. Expert opinion suggests it was probably painted for the Dominican monastery at Thetford. Thornham Parva parish decided in the 1990s to have it restored and it returned to the church in 2003. Viewing it from left to right, the pictures in the arcades are as follows: St Dominic, St Catherine, St John the Baptist, St Peter, the crucifixion, St Paul, St Edmund, St Margaret of Antioch and St Peter the Martyr, who was a Dominican friar. They are well balanced, with four saints standing each side of the crucifixion. The panelling beneath the retable is early seventeenth century and was reputedly made from an old pulpit.

UGGESHALL – ST MARY

Uggeshall lies just over a mile west of the A12, and just east of the A145. The church is normally locked but a key-holder lives nearby.

Reed thatched roofs cover both the nave and the chancel, with scallops and points ornamenting their ridges. The chancel ridge is at a higher level than that of the nave; often with thatched churches the reverse is found.

It is constructed mainly of flint and brick, with some nineteenth-century weatherboarding on the small belfry that tops the west tower stump. Another thatched roof caps the belfry and again scallops and points decorate its ridge. The tower stump walls consist of flint and are heavily buttressed. Below the west window an inscription requests prayers for John Jewle and his wife, who probably once contributed towards the construction cost.

The nave dates from the Norman era and the arch over the blocked north doorway is still visible. A porch, also with a thatched roof, shelters the Norman south doorway. Whitewash now covers the exterior walls of the nave, which contain mainly two-light windows, with a single lancet immediately west of the porch. The chancel dates from the fourteenth century but its east wall was reconstructed during the eighteenth century, in brick-and-flint chequer work. The Victorians carried out a later restoration.

Inside the church is an octagonal font, ornamented with lions, angels and flowers. The pulpit is Jacobean and there are a few remnants of a wall painting opposite the south doorway, the usual position for a St Christopher. The Victorians were responsible for the introduction of the elaborately decorated pipe organ and also for much of the good quality stained glass in the windows. The east window was restored in 1987. The three-light stained-glass window depicting the Madonna and child was installed in 2001 and is attributed to Rachel Thomas, a Somerset artist.

Westhall – St Andrew

This church lies just off the B1124, about 4 miles north-east of Halesworth. A signpost in Westhall village points to it.

It has a small, square south-west tower with embattlements, built of flint, which dates from 1300. It was built in two stages. It has flushwork buttresses and contains five bells. As with many other churches, the rest of the church is a mixture of architectural styles, ranging from Norman to Perpendicular. The south door and tower arch are basically twelfth century, while the chancel and nave were constructed in the middle of the fourteenth century. The south aisle and the Perpendicular windows of the nave are fifteenth century and the north porch dates to the sixteenth century. Before all these developments took place, the original Norman church consisted of just a nave and an apsidal chancel; the nave was converted into the south aisle in the fifteenth century.

Norfolk reed thatch shelters the nave, but the chancel is tiled, as is the porch, which is built of flint and stone. The ridge of the thatch is ornamented with scallops and points, with a decorative thatched apron below. The nave was last rethatched in 1979 and now has a cover of moss on it. Moss normally gathers on the north side of a thatch where it is cooler and shadier; trees exacerbate the problem.

St Andrew, Westhall, Suffolk

On the inside of the tower, there is a well-preserved Norman doorway consisting of four orders of colonnettes, with the arch carved with four-petalled flowers and grotesque heads of beasts. In the past, a little of the base on each side of the doorway had been deliberately chipped away so that the lip of a large bell removed from the tower could be moved through it.

The arcade in the nave consists of five bays with octagonal piers and arches. This leads through to the south aisle and the lady chapel. The roof of the nave is arched brace and restoration has taken place to prevent the spread of deathwatch beetle. The octagonal fifteenth-century font depicts the seven sacraments and the baptism of Christ around the bowl. Other ornamentation includes angels with outstretched wings, images of saints and rosettes in gesso. The oak pulpit dates from the early seventeenth century. The oak eagle lectern was installed in 1919 as a memorial to those locally who died in the First World War. Several fifteenth-century wall paintings have been uncovered in the nave and south aisle. The north wall has a faint painting of St Christopher. The floor is made of bricks.

The benches in the nave have mainly been constructed from timbers obtained from demolished Victorian box pews. However, the oak ones in the south aisle, with poppyheads, may be fifteenth century. Each poppyhead has a small hole in its top; these were once used to hold tapered candles. The choir benches are of uncertain age; the fleur-de-lis of their poppyheads have various carvings, including acorns, berries, haws, plants, animals and birds.

The east five-light window contains fragments of the original mid-fourteenth-century stained glass in the reticulated tracery heads. There is other stained glass in the tracery of the north wall window of the chancel and in the window in the south wall above the choir stall. The sanctuary's stone piscina dates back to the fourteenth century. Nearby stands the sedilia, which is built into the base of the window. The bottom remnants of the screen may be seen at the foot of the chancel arch. It contains sixteen painted panels, eight on either side, depicting thirteen saints with their attributes, and the transfiguration. From north to south, they are: St James the Great, St Leonard, St George, St Clement, the transfiguration with Moses, Salvator Mundi (Christ) and Elijah, St Antony the Great, St Etheldreda, St Zita, St Agnes, St Bridget, St Catherine, St Dorothea, St Margaret of Antioch and St Apollonia. The door in the interior north wall by the screen once led to the stairs of the destroyed rood loft. The Creed and the Lord's Prayer are displayed to the left of the altar and the Commandments to the right. A small white organ stands to the right of the chancel.

Screen dado and east window of St Andrew, Westhall, Suffolk

Westleton – St Peter

This church stands in a large churchyard, which is a wildlife sanctuary. It is located on the B1125, between Blythburgh and Theberton. It is on a rise, close to the green in the centre of the village, with a long path opposite the Crown Inn leading to it.

It has one of the largest thatched roofs in Suffolk. Both the nave and the chancel are thatched with reed, with a parapet wall dividing the two. Scallops and points decorate both ridges. The nave roof was rethatched in 1971 and parts of the chancel roof were done in 2001. Tiles cover the small south porch.

The church, which is built of flints, was completely rebuilt in 1340 by the monks of Sibton. The cross on the top of the east gable wall was added in 1991 to mark its 650th anniversary. The west tower, with its eight bells, fell down in 1776 and only a stump survived. This fell victim to a German landmine during the Second World War. It was dismantled on safety grounds and the base was later roofed and converted into an annexe. A simple archway leads into it from the interior of the church. Instead of the tower, a small bell-cote now stands on the top of the west gable wall and contains a 1960s bell.

The single-aisle church has mainly Y-traceried clear leaded-light

St Peter, Westleton, Suffolk

windows, but two in the chancel are filled with stained glass dating from 1945, which were installed as a thanksgiving for victory in the Second World War. An extremely large five-light window can be seen at the east end, with interlocking Y-tracery. It was rebuilt in 1977 due to decaying stonework and clear glass then installed. This helps to make the interior very light. The white limewash on the interior walls also assists in this respect, as does the cream-coloured brick floor. There are many memorials with ledger slabs in the floor. On the north wall towards its western end, there is a blocked fourteenth-century doorway.

The chancel is exceptionally long. The sanctuary south wall has the original fourteenth-century sedilia and piscina, with four cusped arches above the shafts. The clergy sat on the seats below the three arches that form the sedilia, while the fourth arch sheltered the piscina, where the holy vessels were washed. There is a side altar dedicated to St Francis of Assisi and close by is a niche. The sanctuary also contains an oak coffer behind the oak lectern.

The box pews have small doors for entry and poppyhead finials. Some of them are Victorian, but there are some with medieval tracery. The older ones are the choir stalls to the north. The twentieth-century clergy stall commemorates King George V and has carvings depicting farming and fishing, the main local occupations in those days. The organ in the

Sedilia and piscina in St Peter, Westleton, Suffolk

nave has white pipes; some of the mechanism dates back to the eighteenth century. The nearby octagonal stone font is thought to be fifteenth century. Images of four lions are carved on the stem with a mixture of four lions and four angels on the bowl above. The Victorians installed the pulpit in 1857.

Piracy was once rife in the area and an entry in the churchwardens' accounts for 1731–2, reveals that the sum of 1s 6d was given to a group of seamen who had been captured by pirates and barbarously treated. Outside the church, by the priest's door, lies a large stone that grass will never grow over; it is known as the Witch's Stone. Above it is an iron grating in the wall. Local legend suggests that if someone places a piece of straw in the grating and then runs round the church at least three times, there will be nothing there when they return. However, if the straw has not vanished, the ominous clanging of chains will be heard.

WARWICKSHIRE

Long Compton – St Peter and St Paul

Long Compton is situated 14 miles south of Stratford-upon-Avon directly on the A3400, about 4 miles north-west of Chipping Norton. The church of St Peter and St Paul dates from the thirteenth century and although it is not itself thatched, it is well known for its extremely unusual and charming thatched two-storey lychgate. This once formed the end of a row of 500-year-old cottages; the others were demolished in the early part of the twentieth century. The ground floor now forms the lychgate opening, with the two side walls acting as stilts. The walls are constructed of squared rubble. The thatched roof has a straight ridge ornamented with cross-rods.

The wooden gates across the opening into the churchyard were erected in 1996. They were donated in memory of David Winter Salmon and his wife Katherine Rose Ann, also of Reginald Charles Hunt and his wife Ena Maud, neé Salmon.

The first storey of the lychgate is brick and half-timbered. The underside is wooden planked. It has a squat west chimney and on the opposite gable wall two windows overlook the main road. There is also a large front window. A small thatched west extension is built on to the rear, making an L-shape. A memorial stone on the exterior west gable wall,

Lychgate at St Peter and St Paul, Long Compton, Warwickshire

Rear view of lychgate at St Peter and St Paul, Long Compton, Warwickshire

below the chimney, reveals that Mr George Kinsey Latham rethatched and renovated the lychgate in 1964. He was a local builder and former resident, and his wife Marion donated the memorial to him. The roof has since been rethatched.

The lychgate has a long and varied history; at one time it may have been used by the priest for parish business. It also once served as a small museum and in the 1920s and 1930s it was used as a cobbler's workshop and also as an antique shop. It now houses church property and there is a small garden beside it, cared for by the parishioners.

WILTSHIRE

Chisbury – St Martin's Chapel

This mid-thirteenth-century thatched chapel sits beside an unclassified country lane. An English Heritage signpost along the lane indicates its location ¼ mile east of Chisbury, which is off the A4, 6 miles east of Marlborough. It takes about ten minutes to walk from Chisbury along the east lane. There is no charge to visit the site.

St Martin's Chapel, Chisbury, Wiltshire

St Martin's was originally built as a chapel of ease, a place of worship for the use of parishioners residing at a distance from the parish church of Great Bedwyn. Unfortunately, it was later neglected for many years and became in effect a ruin. It was even once used as a farm building. Fortunately, English Heritage now cares for it. English Heritage instigated the rethatching of the chapel in 1999 by Jonathan Howell, a thatcher from Shaftesbury in Dorset. The material selected for the thatch was long straw and the apex of the roof was finished with a plain flush straw ridge. Wire netting was used to cover the entire surface to prevent bird and wind damage. This is usual for long straw thatch, the traditional material used for thatching in Wiltshire.

The gable-ended rectangular chapel, constructed of flints in the Decorated style, has Saxon-type long-and-short stone quoins at its corners. The hood-moulds over the window spaces show good craftsmanship, with ornamented bosses or labels stops. There is a Gothic type doorway.

Additional work was sanctioned by English Heritage in 2005 to enhance the long-term preservation of the building. This included internal and external plaster conservation, repairs to the earthen floor, conservation of the remaining historic paintwork fragments and the reinstatement of a timber dais at the west end of the chapel. No window glass was placed in the empty window spaces.

Incidentally, the chapel lies beside Chisbury Camp, a circular Iron Age hill-fort with a single embankment, which spreads over approximately 15 acres, about 575 feet above sea level, offering good views over the surrounding countryside.

Horningsham – The Old Meeting House

This thatched Congregational chapel, which was formerly Presbyterian, is situated 1 mile south of Longleat in Chapel Street, Horningsham. It nestles at a lower level than the road. Horningsham is reached off the A362 Warminster to Frome road. The building alongside the chapel was formerly the manse, but was converted into the school house in 1860. The chapel leaflet states, 'The school house will in the future be used for an exhibition on the history of the chapel and Nonconformist worship and traditions.'

Owned by Viscount Weymouth, this is probably the earliest free church in England still used for worship. The date 1566 is carved on a

The Old Meeting House, Horningsham, Wiltshire

large stone block in the gable wall, just below the thatched eaves level and centrally above the two long west windows facing the roadside. The smaller windows on the sides of the chapel are arranged in two tiers.

An early chapel minute book records:

> It is supposed Horningsham Chapel was built in the year 1566/7 at the time Longleat House was erected. A few Scotsmen employed as workmen in the building of Longleat House used to worship God in nearby Penny's Wood. These devoted workmen not having any stated place of worship ultimately obtained permission and Sir John Thynne, it is believed, allowed them at his charge to build a small house in which they might worship God according to their own tenets.

Sir John Thynne, a friend of the Protector Somerset, had bought the site at Longleat, after the dissolution of the monasteries. He paid £53 and it has remained in the same family ever since. However, although it was built in 1566–7 it may have been re-erected later, as it was not licensed as a chapel until 1700. The old chapel minute book further records: 'The license of the Chapel was granted in the reign of William and Mary at Marlborough in 1700 but much to be regretted is lost.' A plaque inside also records this.

The present chapel measures 45 by 27 feet, but it was smaller originally; extensions have taken place since. The walls are mainly of stone rubble, and buttresses now support the south one. The first enlargement took place in 1754 at the east end and a second extension was added in 1816 at the west end. In 1863, the chapel was repaired and refurbished; the old box pews, with their doors and high backs, were dismantled and new pews installed. The original door was also fitted in 1863 and the outline of its former position can still be clearly seen on the outside wall. A further extensive renovation took place in 1935, and it was again repaired and completely re-roofed in 1959–60. It was again rethatched in 1990. The wheat reed roof is topped with a traditional straight flush wire-netted ridge, and the thatch undulates over the eyebrow-type upper tier windows of the chapel.

A Sun insurance plaque still remains above the current entrance door; this was formerly intended to show the firemen that the building was insured and therefore their services would be paid for. An interesting old stone with a very worn inscription can be found on the outside gable wall between the two long windows and below the date stone. A member of the National Council for the Care of Churches managed to decipher the words in 1932. They read:

> In memory of Willm. Barnes who died of Hydrophobia: He was bitten by a Dog on the 18 of May and was Dipped in the Salt Water on the 19 and Died on the 31 July following after a few HOURS of strong PAROXYSMS: aged 28 years 1820.

Sun Insurance plaque on The Old Meeting House, Horningsham, Wiltshire

Inside the chapel, a Georgian oak pulpit stands high on its pedestal. Downstairs there are benches separated by a central aisle; the two side galleries above still have their original pews. Ash pillars support the galleries. Ladies and gentlemen sat facing one another across the chapel; one side of the men's gallery still has a row of hat-pegs fixed to the low ceiling behind but the facing ladies' gallery has none. This type of arrangement possibly gave rise to the saying, 'Her eyes stood out like chapel hat-pegs.'

Interior of The Old Meeting House, Horningsham, Wiltshire

The large-faced clock is over 200 years old, according to the chapel leaflet. It relates that once the cord holding the clock weight broke and four pounds of lead narrowly missed the bald head of a patriarchal worshipper! As a result the clock was taken down but found a new home in a chair factory near the chapel, belonging to a Mr George Thorne. When the factory eventually closed, the deacons retrieved the clock and it was fixed to the top of the gallery out of harm's way.

A service marking the 400th anniversary of the building of Longleat House was held both at the house and the chapel. The specially invited preacher at the chapel was the well-known Methodist minister, the Revd Donald Soper, who died in 1998.

Sandy Lane – Church of St Mary and St Nicholas

This small church is believed to be the only one in England of timber and thatch construction that was originally built as a place of worship. It is situated in a quiet lane at the southern end of the beautiful estate village of Sandy Lane, about 100 yards off the A342 Devizes to Chippenham road, about 1 mile north-east of Chittoe and 4 miles west of Calne.

St Mary and St Nicholas, Sandy Lane, Wiltshire

J. H. Hopkins of Worcester designed the building, which was opened on the Feast of St Nicholas as a mission church on 6 December 1892. Many mission churches at this time were constructed from kits using galvanized iron, so the charming rustic design at Sandy Lane was quite unusual. The total construction cost was about £170 and the fittings a further £50. It is understood that a Miss Wyndham, one of the tenants of the Spye estate, paid the bill. Today, even to rethatch the church would cost in excess of £5,000. The church was originally dedicated to St Nicholas alone but it took taking the name St Mary from the mother church at Chittoe, which was made redundant in 1980. The Bishop of Ramsbury officiated at the rededication, which took place on the Feast of the Conception of the Blessed Virgin Mary, on the 8 December 1981. The church is now a chapel of ease in the new parish, which now includes Bromham, Chittoe and Sandy Lane.

It is attractively thatched with long straw and has a straight ridge, ornamented with parallel liggers and cross-rods; the eaves are also ornamented in this way. The building itself is made entirely of wood. The exterior walls have horizontal timber planks but there is also a cavity timber wall behind. Sawdust fills the 6-inch cavity to improve the insulation. The roof timbers are A-form and there are six pairs of trusses supporting the thatched roof. The naïve wooden buttresses seen outside are an extension of the roof timbers and at ground level are tensioned to the base of the church walls. The absence of adequate damp-proofing in Victorian times has inevitably led to some rotting of the basic timber structure and funds are constantly needed to prevent further deterioration.

The non-cruciform church is entered through a protruding wooden porch sheltered by a separate thatched roof that joins up to the main roof. Inside there is a central aisle with benches each side, and a wooden rood screen divides the nave from the chancel. Wood dominates the church, including the rectangular plain leaded-light windows with tracery, the floor and the plank ceiling. The octagonal font and the carved lectern are also constructed of wood; the only exceptions are the nineteenth-century brass oil lamps hanging from the ceiling, which have now been converted to electricity. The organ came from the redundant church of St Mary's at Chittoe. It is operated by a wooden handle and is a pump pipe organ by Bevington and Sons of Soho, London. It was installed in 1983.

The churchyard is peaceful and serene, and it is carefully managed to encourage wild flowers, butterflies and birds. Areas of grass are left

Chancel of St Mary and St Nicholas, Sandy Lane, Wiltshire

Organ in St Mary and St Nicholas, Sandy Lane, Wiltshire

unmowed, allowing flowers to seed and butterflies to breed. Gravestones and walls remain untouched to preserve the mosses and lichens growing on them. The trees and shrubs provide food and shelter for the birds and insects.

Bibliography

AA Book of British Villages (Drive Publications, 1980)

AA Illustrated Guide to Country Towns and Villages of Britain (Drive Publications, 1985)

Betjeman, J., *John Betjeman's Guide to English Parish Churches* (Harper Collins, 1993)

Billett, M.G., *The Complete Guide to Living with Thatch* (Robert Hale, 2003)

Blue Guide: Churches and Chapels, Southern England (A & C Black, 1991)

Brabbs, D., *England's Heritage* (Cassell, in association with English Heritage, 2001)

Brabbs, D., *English Country Churches* (George Weidenfeld and Nicholson, 1985)

Brown, R.J., *English Village Architecture* (Robert Hale, 2004)

Brown, R.J., *The English Village Church* (Robert Hale, 1998)

Churches in Retirement: A Gazetteer (HMSO, 1990)

Clifton-Taylor, A., *English Parish Churches* (Oxford University Press, 1989)

Cooper, J.C., *An Illustrated Encyclopaedia of Traditional Symbols* (Thames and Hudson, 1978)

Farmer, D., *Oxford Dictionary of Saints* (Oxford University Press, 1997)

Grigson, G., *The Shell Country Alphabet* (Michael Joseph and Rainbird, 1966)

Hall, J., *Hall's Dictionary of Subjects and Symbols in Art* (John Murray, 1974)

Harbison, R., *The Shell Guide to English Parish Churches* (André Deutsch, 1992)

Harris, J. and Lever, J., *Illustrated Glossary of Architecture 850–1830* (Faber and Faber, 1966)

Harrod, W., *The Norfolk Guide* (The Alastair Press, 1988)

Jenkins, S., *England's Thousand Best Churches* (Penguin Books, 1999)

Kinross, J., *Discovering England's Smallest Churches* (Weidenfeld and Nicolson, 2003)

Pevsner, N., *The Buildings of England* (Penguin Books, various volumes)
St Mary's Church, Thornham Parva, Suffolk: A Guide to the Wall Paintings (The Courtauld Institute of Art, 1989)
Scarfe, N., *The Suffolk Guide* (The Alastair Press, 1988)
Shell Guide to England (Michael Joseph and Rainbird, 1970)
Smith, E and Cook, O., *English Parish Churches* (Thames and Hudson, 1976)
Smith, I., *Tin Tabernacles* (Camroie Organization, 2004)
Young, G., *Country Churches* (George Philip, 1991)

Glossary

Abacus The flat slab on the top of a capital.

Apron The thatch layer below a block-cut ridge, sometimes finished with spars and liggers. Also used as ornamentation under chimneys and windows that are set in the roof.

Apse Semicircular or polygonal end of a chancel.

Arcade A range of arches supported on piers or columns.

Arched brace A roof truss with curved braces to help strengthen the tie-beam or collar-beam.

Architrave The lowest of the main parts of the entablature.

Aumbry A recess in the wall of a church to keep the sacred vessels.

Bell-cote A turret designed to hold bells, usually on the west end of the roof of a towerless church. A sanctus bell-cote is one normally located over the chancel arch in the church and the bell is rung at the consecration of the host.

Billet An ornamentation used in Norman architecture. It consists of short cylindrical or rectangular blocks or billets, placed in hollow mouldings at regular intervals.

Bole The trunk of a tree or wood log.

Capital The uppermost part of a column.

Castellated With battlements.

Censer A vessel for the burning of incense.

Chamfer The surface made by cutting across the square angle of a stone block, usually at an angle of 45° to the other two surfaces.

Chancel The eastern part of a church, in which the altar and choir stalls are situated. Sometimes a screen separates it from the nave.

Chantry chapel An endowed chapel in which prayers were said for the benefactor.

Chapel A separate building or a small area with an altar set aside for worship within a church.

Chapel of ease A place of worship convenient for parishioners residing at a distance from the parish church.

Chevron A Norman zigzag pattern.

Choir The area nearest the nave inside the chancel, used by the choir and clergy.

Classical Architectural styles inspired by the Greeks and Romans.

Clerestory The upper storey of the nave above the aisle roofs and fitted with windows to light the interior.

Cob A mixture of clay, straw, gravel and sand, or sometimes mud, straw, animal dung and horsehair.

Collar-beam A horizontal beam high in the roof structure joining the opposite principal rafters and forming with them an A-shape.

Colonnette A small column.

Combed wheat reed Wheat straw that has been passed through a reed comber.

Consecration cross A cross inside a circle, placed on the exterior and interior walls of a church, in medieval times as a defence against the Devil. Bishops consecrated newly built or rebuilt churches with one.

Cornice A moulded projection used as a decorative feature along the upper section of a wall, door or window.

Cottage ornée A small building constructed to capture the rustic style of the vernacular, a manifestation of the picturesque.

Course A horizontal layer of reed or straw thatch.

Crocket A carved projection in leaf form, placed at regular intervals to decorate the edges of pinnacles, gables and spires.

Cross-rods Split and crossed hazel rods used for fixing and decoration between liggers on a thatched roof; also known as cross-stitches.

Crow-step A stepped side to a gable.

Cruciform In the shape of a cross.

Cusp The point that projects between the foils or arcs in a Gothic arch or tracery.

Decalogue The Ten Commandments.

Decorated A stylistic phase of English Gothic architecture that developed from the end of the thirteenth century to the middle of the fourteenth century. It is characterized by the complex tracery of the windows, which undulates and interweaves.

Dentil One of a series of small rectangular blocks arranged similarly to a row of teeth.

Diagonal buttress A buttress placed at the angle formed by the meeting of two perpendicular walls.

Early English A stylistic phase of English Gothic architecture of the thirteenth century. Lancet windows without tracery form a characteristic feature.

Easter sepulcre A recess in the north chapel that holds an effigy of the risen Christ during Easter.

Entablature In classical architecture, the whole of all the horizontal parts above a column.

Fan vault A vault composed of inverted concave cones overlaid with numerous ribs of the same curvature and length, radiating at equal angles from one springer, producing a fan-like pattern.

Finial Ornamentation on top of a gable, canopy, pinnacle or carved top of a bench end.

Flushwork The decorative use of flint in conjunction with dressed stone to form wall patterns, commonly found in East Anglia.

Foil Each of the small arc openings separated by cusps in Gothic tracery.

Font A large raised basin containing holy water for baptisms.

Frieze The part of an entablature between the architrave and the cornice.

Gallery An upper storey above an aisle opened in arches to the nave and sometimes called the tribune. Also a projecting balcony that overlooks the nave.

Gesso Gypsum used to make plaster in sculpture or painting.

Gnomon The rod or pin in the centre of a sundial.

Gothic The style that dominated English architecture after the Norman or Romanesque, until the sixteenth century. It is characterized by the pointed arch and the vault. The English Gothic period is subdivided into Early English, Decorated and Perpendicular.

Hood-mould A projecting moulding over an opening, such as a window or door to throw off rainwater. Also called a dripstone.

Instruments of the passion The numerous objects that occur in the story of the passion, such as the crown of thorns, nails and lance; there are many others.

Ionic One of the three Greek orders, characterized by volutes on the capitals and dentils in the cornices, with fluted shafts.

Iron hooks or crooks An iron rod of ¼ inch diameter and varying in length from 8 to 12 inches, pointed at one end like a nail and with a right-angle hook at the other to hold a sway down over thatch.

Jacobean An architectural style popular during the reign of James I (1603–25), with a trend towards using purer classical forms.

Lady chapel A chapel within a church dedicated to the Virgin Mary.

Lancet A tall and narrow pointed window, characteristic of the Early English period.

Lectern A reading stand on the right-hand side of a church designed to hold a bible.

Ledger A slab laid over interments in the floor of a church, especially in the chancel. Usually of black marble but local stone, slate and iron are also used.

Ligger A long length of split hazel or willow that is pegged down with spars into thatch. Used on the ridges of water reed and combed wheat reed roofs to secure and decorate them. Additionally used on long straw roofs to hold in and ornament the eaves and verges.

Linenfold panelling A form of carved Tudor panelling, ornamented with a conventional representation of a piece of linen laid in vertical folds.

Linhay A rustic building with an open front, often thatched and used for stabling horses.

Long-and-short work Saxon quoins, in which flat horizontal slabs alternate with tall vertical ones.

Long straw Threshed wheat straw prepared by hand for thatching; it is wetted to make it more pliable before making into bundles, called yealms.

Louvre A window opening covered with overlapping boards.

Lychgate A roofed gateway to a churchyard, where a bier awaits the clergyman's arrival to lead it into consecrated ground and later burial.

Misericord A bracket on the underside of a hinged choir stall seat which, when turned up, provides a support for the clergy during long periods of standing during a service. Often carved with animals and allegorical figures and also called a miserere.

Nave The main area of the church used by the congregation, extending from the entrance to the transept, choir or chancel.

Nonconformist A member of a sect dissenting from the Anglican Church.

Ogee arch A pointed arch, formed of two convex arcs above and two concave arcs below. The shape became especially popular in the fourteenth century.

Pediment A low-pitched triangular gable in classical and neo-classical architecture, usually above a portico but also used as an ornamental feature above doors and windows.

Perpendicular English Gothic architecture covering the period 1335 to around 1530. The strong vertical lines of its tracery form a distinguishing feature.

Pier A strong solid support, usually square in section.

Pinnacle A small, pointed, pyramidal or conical stone ornament on top of a buttress, parapet, tower, spire or gable; crockets often decorate it.

Piscina Shallow bowl with drain for washing sacred vessels; generally set in a niche, south of the altar. When free-standing on a pillar, it is called a pillar piscina.

Poppyhead The ornamental finial of a bench end often carved with leaf and flower motifs, such as fleur-de-lis; also sometimes carved with animals and figures.

Portico A covered colonnade forming a central entrance to a church or building.

Priest's door A small door leading into the chancel, giving an independent access for the clergy and usually on the south side of the church.

Pulpit A raised enclosed platform on the left-hand side of a church used to preach the sermon.

Purbeck marble Not a true marble but a hard fossilized limestone, derived from freshwater snails, mined in the Isle of Purbeck, Dorset, and widely used in churches during the thirteenth century.

Purlin A longitudinal timber in the roof parallel to the wall.

Quatrefoil Four foils.

Queenpost A type of roof with two vertical struts placed symmetrically on a tie-beam, rising to the junction of collar beam, purlin and principal rafter.

Quoins Dressed stones at the external angles of a building.

Raggle The residual marks on a wall, indicating the line of a former roof.

Reredos An ornamented structure behind and above the altar.

Retable An altarpiece, picture or carving standing behind and attached to the altar.

Ridge The apex of a roof; a thatched one is capped with an additional layer of straw or sedge.

The main types are:

a) Plain: flush to the roof surface with minimal decoration.

b) Decorated: also flush but decorated with cross-rods or a herringbone pattern.

c) Straight cut block: 3–4 inches thick above the roof surface and cut in a straight line below the bottom ligger.

d) Ornamented cut block: as above but with the bottom edge cut into scallops and points or other patterns.

Rood Statues of Mary the Virgin and St John the Evangelist flanking the Christ crucified on the beam of the rood screen. Most were destroyed during the Reformation.

Rood loft A gallery above the rood screen, accessed by stairs for lighting candles.

Rood screen A carved wooden screen separating the chancel from the nave and built below the rood loft, on which the rood or crucifix was placed.

Sacristy A room in or attached to a church, where the sacred vessels and vestments are kept.

Saddleback A tower roof in which the top takes the form of an ordinary roof gable. A double saddleback is a roof with two gables, lying side by side along their lengths.

Sanctuary The most sacred part of a church around the main altar. It once provided fugitives from the law with immunity from arrest.

Scallop A curved decorative shape cut under a thatched ridge of a roof in the form of a scallop.

Scratch dial A sundial on the south wall of a church that casts the sun's shadow, via a gnomon, on to scratch marks on the wall.

Screen The chancel screen, usually of wood that separates the chancel from the nave; if a cross sits on top it is called a rood screen.

Sedge A marsh grass used for ridge construction on a water reed roof.

Sedilia Three seats for priest, deacon and sub-deacon on the south side of the chancel. Often recessed into the wall at three different levels, sometimes with carved canopies above.

Shingle A thin rectangular wedge-shaped piece of wood used as a roof tile.

Sounding-board Horizontal board or canopy over a pulpit to resonate the clergy's voice, also known as a tester.

Spandrel A triangular surface contained by one side of an arch by a horizontal drawn from its apex and a vertical drawn from its springing. Also the surface between two adjacent arches and the horizontal moulding or string cornice above them.

Spar A split hazel rod, pointed at each end and twisted in the centre into a U-shape which, when thrust into thatch over a ligger or sway, holds down one layer of thatch on another.

Splay The jamb of a window constructed so that the opening is widened from the window to the face of the interior wall, to allow more light to enter.

Springing The point at which an arch rises from its support.

Stoup A vessel for holy water for the use of the congregation as they entered the church. They were often carved into a wall and usually placed near the church door.

Sway A long rod made of hazel, willow or now often steel, laid across a course of thatch to secure it to the rafters. Sways are fixed with hooks driven into the rafter, or attached with screw ties or tarred twine. The sways are hidden when the next course of thatch is laid over them.

Tester Horizontal board or canopy over a pulpit, also known as a sounding-board.

Thatch Straw, water reed, heather, turf, broom or gorse used as a roof covering.

Tie-beam A horizontal beam spanning the space from wall-plate to wall-plate to prevent the walls spreading.

Tracery Ornamented intersecting ribwork in the upper part of a window. Various common types include plate, bar, geometric, Y, intersecting, reticulated and panel.

Transept North and south of the crossing, where the nave and chancel meet, forming the transverse arm of a cruciform church.

Transfiguration The occasion on Mount Tabor in Galilee when Christ manifested his divine nature by becoming transfigured in the presence of the disciples Peter, James and John. His face shone and a voice from heaven said, 'This is my son.'

Truss A scrolled bracket.

Tympanum The space between the lintel of a doorway and the arch above it.

Vault An arched roof or ceiling.

Vestry A room in or attached to a church where vestments are kept and where the clergy and choir robe.

Volute A spiral scroll.

Wall-plate A timber laid longitudinally along the top of a wall.

Water reed A wetland plant used as thatch material.

Wheat reed Wheat straw that has been passed through a comber.

Saints to Whom Thatched Churches Are Dedicated

Saint	Description	Feast Day
All Saints	Those believed to be in heaven; it includes all saints known or unknown.	1 Nov
St Agnes	Virgin martyr of Rome, put to death by the sword *c.* 305, for her refusal to marry because of her dedication to Christ.	21 Jan
St Andrew	Former fisherman who became an apostle of Christ and took a prominent part in the feeding of the 5,000. Later, he was martyred and put to death by crucifixion, *c.* 60. His attribute is a cross in the shape of an X, known as the Saltire cross.	30 Nov
St Botolph (St Botulf)	Born in East Anglia; he built monastery at Iken, in Suffolk in 654. He became one of the early founders of Benedictine monasticism in England. He died *c.* 680.	17 June
St Edmund	King of East Anglia, captured by invading Vikings. He became a martyr by refusing to deny his Christian faith and was shot with arrows, before being beheaded in 869. A wolf reputedly guarded his severed head until it was retrieved by his followers.	20 Nov
St Ethelbert	King of East Anglia and martyr. Met a violent death in 794 at the instigation of Offa, King of Mercia, for political reasons.	20 May

Saint	Description	Feast Day
St Fabian	Became Pope in 236 and reorganized the Church until he was martyred in 250, when persecution arose in Rome. His body was later entombed in the church of St Sebastian, with whom he shares a feast day.	20 Jan
St Felix	A missionary bishop from Normandy, who arrived in East Anglia *c.* 630, at the request of King Sigebert, to bring the Christian faith to the people of Norfolk. Died in 647.	8 Mar
St Francis of Assisi	Italian friar born in Assisi and founder of the Franciscan Order. He renounced worldly wealth in 1205 to live in poverty and devote himself to prayer and charitable work. He was reported to be the first saint to receive the stigmata, the marks of wounds similar to those of Christ, in 1224. He died in 1226 and due to his close affinity with animals and birds became the patron saint of ecology in 1980.	4 Oct
St George	Patron saint of England and soldiers. Crusaders introduced his cult to England, after returning from Palestine. He suffered at Lydda in Palestine and was martyred there. In 303, after enduring poison, being stretched on a wheel and placed in a boiling cauldron, he was beheaded. In legend, he is famous for slaying a dragon to rescue a maiden. The dragon symbolizes the evil of Satan and the triumph of good and Christianity over it.	23 Apr
St Gregory	One of the four Latin doctors of the Church, also known as Gregory the Great. He helped to lay the foundation of	3 Sept

Saint	Description	Feast Day
	Christianity in England when the pope introduced the rule of celibacy for the clergy. He died *c*. 604.	
St James	The apostle known as James the Great, to distinguish him from James the Less. James the Great was the brother of John the Evangelist and was one of the three witnesses of the transfiguration of Christ. He was the first apostle to die for his faith, put to the sword at Jerusalem in AD 44.	25 July
St James the Less	Usually described as 'the Lord's brother', but with uncertainty. He was sentenced to death by the Sanhedrin in AD 62. He was stoned and died after being beaten with a fuller's club.	1 May
St John the Baptist	Son of Zacharias and Elizabeth, a cousin of the Virgin Mary, whose birth was foretold by the angel Gabriel. He was the forerunner of Jesus Christ. He preached about the coming Messiah and baptized Christ in the River Jordan. Herod ordered his head to be severed and then presented to Salome, at her request *c*. 30.	24 June, & 29 Aug for his beheading
St Lawrence (St Laurence)	Roman deacon reputedly martyred in 258 by being roasted on a gridiron during the reign of Emperor Valerian. He was renowned for the giving of alms.	10 Aug
St Leonard	A Benedictine monk who later became a hermit in the 500s. Remigius had converted him to Christianity. He became the patron saint of prisoners and was known for the power of his prayer to assist women in childbirth.	6 Nov

Saint	Description	Feast Day
St Margaret	A legendary virgin martyr, known as Margaret of Antioch, date unknown, who became one of the most popular saints. Legend relates that she refused to marry the prefect of Antioch, declaring she was a Christian virgin. She was thrown into prison where Satan, in the form of a dragon, devoured her. The cross she held in her hand caused the dragon to burst asunder and she emerged unharmed. She was later beheaded and eventually became the patron saint of childbirth.	20 July
St Martin	A patron saint of France, Bishop of Tours and a former soldier in the Roman army. He was distinguished by the image of cutting his cloak in half to give one half to a beggar in Amiens. The following night, he dreamed he saw Christ wearing the donated half of his cloak in heaven. He was baptized soon afterwards. He died *c*. 397.	11 Nov
St Mary	The Blessed Virgin, the mother of Jesus Christ.	
St Matthias	One of the apostles who preached in Judea and further afield. In the first century AD, he was martyred with an axe or halberd (a combined spear and battleaxe).	24 Feb
St Michael	An archangel and leader of the angels who cast out the dragon or Satan from heaven. As a result, St Michael's churches are traditionally built on hilltops. He is responsible for the weighing of souls at the last judgement.	29 Sept

Saint	Description	Feast Day
St Nicholas	Bishop of Myra in Turkey in AD 4, who became widely known for his legendary gifts. He became the patron saint of Russia, sailors and children. In one of the legends, he gave three bags of gold to three girls for their marriage dowries, in order to rescue them from prostitution. The institution of Santa Claus was due to him because of his gifts to children.	6 Dec
St Paul	The apostle, born Saul of Tarsus, a Jew who experienced a vision of Christ on the road to Damascus. He was converted to Christianity and spread the faith amongst the Gentiles. He wrote a major part of the New Testament. He was beheaded *c.* 65, under Nero's rule.	29 June
St Peter	A fisherman on the Sea of Galilee who became one of the twelve apostles and their leader. However, his faith wavered after Christ's arrest, and he denied him three times. Christ told him that he would be the rock on which the Church would be built and he was symbolically given the keys to the kingdom of Heaven. He was martyred and crucified upside down, according to tradition, *c.* 64.	29 June
St Remigius	Bishop of Reims, who converted and baptized Clovis I, King of the Franks. He died in 533.	1 Oct, & 13 Jan at Reims
St Sebastian	A Roman martyr, who legend relates was an officer of the Praetorian Guards until the Emperor Diocletian discovered he was a Christian and ordered that he be shot with arrows. However, he did not die and was later beaten to death with clubs *c.* 300.	20 Jan

Saint	**Description**	**Feast Day**
St Stephen	The first Christian martyr, according to the New Testament. He was appointed by the apostles to provide charity to Christian widows. He became a preacher and was accused of blasphemy, for which the Jews stoned him to death, *c.* AD 35.	26 Dec
St Thomas of Canterbury	Archbishop and martyr, born Thomas à Becket, who became Henry II's chancellor in 1154. He later quarrelled with Henry and resigned. On Henry's orders, he was murdered in Canterbury Cathedral on 29 December 1170.	29 Dec
Trinity	The Father, the Son and the Holy Ghost.	

Index